D1524218

MAN AND ENVIRONMENT IN NORTHEAST INDIA

Volume - III

To
Professor Carla Sinopoli
with compliments

Sept 10, 2008

MAN AND ENVIRONMENT IN NORTHEAST INDIA

Volume - III

Heritage Issue I

Anthropology, Archaeology and Heritage

Editor

Dilip K. Medhi

B.Sc. (Honours- B.S. Guha Medalist)
M.Sc. (Anthropology – Gold Medalist, Gauhati University)
Ph.D. (Archaeology, Deccan College, Pune)
Fellow of Asian Cultural Council, New York
Professor and Heritage Expert

Editorial Board

EBH Publishers (India)
Guwahati

Man and Environment in Northeast India, Volume III, Heritage Issue # I *(Anthropology, Archaeology and Heritage) is aimed at giving an insight into the art and culture of Northeast India, which is long been considered as a little known territory of the World. After the successful production of Volumes I & II in the year of 1993 and 2002 respectively, this Volume will highlight the enormously rich art and cultural resources of Northeast India or the Assam Region into the knowledge of academicians in India and abroad as well. It is 3rd in the series of a project that Dilip K. Medhi initiated and conceived in the eighties of last Century.*

Logo: Designed by Darpan Kaustuv Medhi (*Dol*) and Dilip K. Medhi with initial assistance from Dilip Changkakati

First Edition, 2008

Published by:
EBH PUBLISHERS (India)
is an imprint of
Eastern Book House
136, M.L. Nehru Road
Panbazar, Guwahati 781 001
Ph.   91-361-2513876,   2519231,   09954705692
Fax: 91-361-2519231
e-mail:info@easternbookhouse.com
web:www.easternbookhouse.com

ISBN 81-9038-349-3

Composed by:
Darpan Kaustuv Medhi
University of Sheffiled, U.K.

Type setting at: EBH Publishers (India)
Printed in India at: *Genesis*

iii

FOREWORD

Richard a. Engelhardt

What is now referred to as Northeast India comprises the area formerly known for centuries as *Assam*. This region is situated between the Chinese landmass on the north, the Southeast Asian river valleys on the east and the Indian sub-continent on the west. With the Brahamaputra River running through it, this region has for millennia been a corridor for the passage of animals and men; for armies and ideas. Dr. Dilip K. Medhi in his own words defines Assam as the 'Great Indian Corridor in the East'; a passage for the migration of people to and from China, Southeast Asia and mainland India. Geography and history explain why today the region embraces a diverse population whose elaborate cultures draw and mix traits from all three neighbouring regions. The awesome beauty and bountiful climate surely were powerful attractions to the many different ethnic communities who came to this region. A Subtropical warm and humid climate with maximum precipitation keeps the hills green. The Brahmaputra, one of the largest rivers in the world, waters the region, flowing from China through the plains of Assam in between the Northern Himalayas and the Southern Hills.

The strategic importance of Northeast India (or the Assam Region) to the understanding of human cultures is, however, a topic that is not yet appreciated by the scholarly world at large, because it has not yet attracted the research attention it should.

Dr. Medhi is making a valiant attempt to bring historic Assam to the attention of the scholarly world through a series of volumes entitled "Man and Environment in Northeast India". He has already completed two volumes and now has published a most welcome third volume in the series devoted specifically to culture heritage issues.

I have enjoyed a long association with Dr. Medhi whom I met through our membership in the Indo-Pacific Prehistory Association. Through our association, I have had the privilege to make several research visits to Northeast India into the present Indian States of Assam, Meghalaya, Manipur and Arunchal Pradesh. Dr. Medhi's passion to bring to light the cultural heritage of Northeast India is inspiring. From the Nortiang Prehistoric Megaliths to the Neo-Vaishnavite Sattra Culture of Majuli River Island, Dr. Medhi's pursuit of the cultural history of the region is as tireless as it is wide-ranging.

This Heritage Issue of "Man and Environment in Northeast India" comprises seven articles on different key heritage issues in Northeast India. Dr. Medhi leads the volume with his own contribution entitled: 'Introducing the Culture Heritage of Northeast India' in which he attempts to identify the different culture areas of Northeast India through a study of personal material culture such as jewelry and other ornamentation. (This is a theme which will be carried into Volume 4 of the series.)

The second article in this volume is a presentation by the Late Professor Maheswar Neog on Saint Sankardeva. This article tells about the life and religion of the great Saint who founded the Neo-Vaishnavite religious culture of Assam. Professor Neog was the leading authority on Saint Sankardeva and therefore provides the reader with a definitive study on the Saint, which will stand for years to come.

Dr. Sujit Choudhury writes in his article about the legendary 'Bhuban Hill' in the Surma Valley in Cachar District of Assam State. From time immemorial, the hill has attracted a wide range of Hindu devotees to the existing shrine on the hilltop. The identification of the people who developed the Bhuban Hill sanctuary is the key issue discussed by Dr. Choudhury in his learned article.

Dr. Pradip C. Sarma writes on 'Temple Architecture in Assam'. He identifies the places of temple origin with their probable foundation dates. Before the spread of the Neo-Vaishnavite religion of Saint Sanakardeva in 15th century, the Assam Region had a number of temple structures built with patronage of the royal families and wealthy merchants of Assam. Included in the study are the famous now-ruined temples of Bamuni Pahar and Dah Parbatia at Tezpur, of Deo Parbat, Negheriting near Jorhat and other temples at Sibsagar. Together they reflect religious concepts embodied in architecture amalgamating the indigenous Tai Ahom style combined with elements from the earlier Gupta Style and the concurrent Mughal Period.

Mr. Promod Goswami, a former United Nation's official in the agricultural sector, discusses the natural heritage of Assam's forests and wildlife. Northeast India is in the Subtropical warm climatic zone of Asia whose characteristic vegetation is the preferred habitat of many varieties of large herbivores, such as the endangered one-horned rhinoceros. It is not surprising that these impressive animals figure prominently in the mythology and iconography of the region's cultures, as well as in their repertory of medicines, food and for other economic uses.

Dr. Biswanarayan Shastri writes on the important *Purâna* tradition in the life of the people of Assam. Myth, legend and stories are contained in the different *Purâna* epics of India which are very popular in the Northeast. Dr. Shastri glosses his discussion with frequent references to Sanskrit sources.

The cultic role of the temple dancer is prevalent throughout India. Assam had a similar institution of it own headquartered at the 'Dubi Temple' near Pathsala which from there spread to other places. Dr. Jibon Krishna Patra writes on the local institution of the temple dancer, popularly known as *Devadâsi* in most of India, but referred to as *Natis* in Assam. Today the Assamese tradition of *Natis* is no longer practiced, but the memory remains of beautiful young girls dancing in front of the temple deity under guidance of elderly musicians.

Dr. Medhi is undoubtedly one of the great guardians of the heritage of Northeast India. With his background in the academic fields of anthropology and archaeology he is well suited to the task of bringing together the many diverse strands of the region's heritage and to weave them into the fabric of our understanding. Although Northeast India is still a relatively remote and isolated region, the impact of modernization and globalization are relentless. Cultures inevitably change, and in the process of moving forward into the future, we rely on the guardians of local cultures everywhere to preserve for us the memory of what has been and where we come from. Dr. Medhi's contribution to this effort through the publication of these scholarly volumes on the cultural heritage of Northeast India is immeasurable.

Dr. Richard a. Engelhardt holds the position of UNESCO Regional Advisor for Culture in Asia and the Pacific at UNESCO Regional Office at Bangkok, Thailand. Dr. Engelhardt vilated Assam and Meghalaya with a 21-day programme at the invitation of Dr. Dilip. K. Medhi. His maiden trip to Majuli River Island was much significant towards a proposed status of 'UNESCO Heritage Site' to the Island.

Editor's Note

My joining graduate Honours Courses in Anthropology in Cotton College, Guwahati in 1967 was a turning point in bringing out this project of producing a series of volume on Man and Environment in Northeast India because it realized me the importance of the erstwhile Assam in the field of anthropological and archaeological studies. Our teachers cited to us several examples and illustrations from Africa, Pacific Islands and America in our lessons, and I did understand the vast reservoir of similar information from Assam. We studied Geography in our early education in Primary to High School standard and so I did learn about the land and the people of the region, and this knowledge in me gave me a projected acquaintance in respect of anthropological studies of the region. I joined Gauhati University for my Master's degree in Anthropology and completed it with similar experience. Meanwhile I did three field studies, one amongst the *Mikirs* (now *Karbis*) from 1968-70, another with the *Rongdani Rabhas* surrounded by the *Boro*, the *Garos*, the *Koch-Rajbongshi* and the *Hajong* in 1970, and finally in the Garo Hills amongst the *Garos* during 1971-1972. All these studies of tribal communities enabled me to get first hand knowledge regarding the primitive culture of the people. Earlier I had a long association with the *Boro Kacharis* of my native place, Bhawanipur in Barpeta besides my archetypal rural life. Later on I had the opportunity of conducting a number of field studies for our undergraduate students during my teaching career from 1973-2004. On every occasion of a field study I remember Late Professor D.N. Majumder whom myself along with many in the field of anthropology consider as the foremost anthropologist of the last Century in India. Professor Majumder is popularly known as D.N. Majumder Jr. in India and abroad. I learnt many things in Anthropology from him after my anthropological fieldwork in 1970 in the Garo Hills with him and Professor M.N. Phookan along with a prolonged association of studentship with them.

The present Volume in the series of Man and Environment in Northeast India figuring as 'Heritage Issue # 1' is one of my humble attempts to explore the little known territories of Assam Region in the fileds of Anthropology, Archaeology and Heritage. In fact this be a long cherished academic venture of mine that I started in the seventies of last Century. For a meaningful production of this series I moved from pillar to stone with lot of mixed experience when my own teacher refused to contribute any article to the Volume I. However I was ready to confront any eventuality and at that point of time, Dr. Thaneswar Sarma, a Professor of Sanskrit and a friend of mine at Gauhati University congratulated me for taking up the project and sent me a Card. Finally I could see the day of my success on December 06, 1993 when the 'first-cum-introductory volume' was released with a beautiful speech presented by Shri Madan Jha, Vice-Chancellor of Arunachal University in the presence of a number of dignitaries including Dr. N.K. Choudhury, then Vice-Chancellor of Gauhati University, Dr. Md. Taher, Dr. Dulal Goswami, Dr. A.C. Bhagbati, Dr. Gopal Bordoloi, Dr. Phani Deka, Dr. Ajit Neog and others at a small and tidy function at Hotel Prag Continental, Panbazar, Guwahati. Shri Jha spoke much eloquently; everybody enjoyed his talk about a topic on man and environment. My third elder brother Late Surendra Nath Medhi who was a Senior Advocate of Supreme Court of India and a politician was also present on that occasion. Shri Ramesh Kumar Virmani and Shri Satish Kumar Virmani, owner of Omsons Publications, Panabazar and ix

New Delhi hosted a dinner to celebrate the occasion. The function began with lighting of earthen lamps by the guests present. On 7th morning Shri Jha joined me at a breakfast at my invitation, and me, my wife Anju, our two kids Pol and Dol along with our family friend Shri Zahid Husein enjoyed the occasion with great enthusiasm. I am happy to tell everybody that the Volume was well received by the academic World. When the second Volume containing eight of my personal articles was

3, Rochester Terrace
Edinburgh   EH10 5AA
Scotland
2.5.93

Dear Dr.Medhi ,

It was most kind of you to send me a copy of your first volume on "Man and Environment", which reached me about three weeks ago. It does not surprise me that the preparation of the book has taken longer than you anticipated, for the work must have involved much energy and effort on your part, not least in securing the cooperation of so many distinguished scholars. It is a privilege to have had the opportunity of contributing the foreword.

You have certainly gathered a wide and very useful collection of articles for this first volume. I have been reading them during the past few days and found them full of interest, learning much that I did not know before. I must congratulate you on this timely and important enterprise. I hope you will be able to continue with the production of further volumes and successfully enlist the cooperation of other scholars.

To receive this book naturally brings back to memory those fascinating years I spent in N.E.India, including a very stimulating period as V.C. of Gauhati University. I trust the University continues to prosper. My wife and I made many friends, and are still in touch with some of them. We send our warmest good wishes to you and your colleagues.

With kind regards,
Yours sincerely,

H.J.Taylor

published in 2003, a teacher of mine who refused to contribute in the first volume pointing at my capabilities asked me whether I brought out a print out of the Volume II I concentrated myself upon the need of the students of anthropology and archaeology, and brought out articles on specific component of courses in syllabi in them. I therefore look forward to receiving good response from the students and teachers of the two disciplines. Professor W.G. Solheim II, former Professor of archaeology in the Department of Anthropology at the University of Hawaii at Manoa, Honolulu, USA and currently working as a Cosultant Professor of Archaeology Prgramme in the Philippine University, Dilman, Quezon City wrote an excellent 'foreword' to the volume II with an appreciation to the entire production.

I am proud to quote a letter of Dr. H.J. Taylor, former Vice-Chancellor, Gauhati University, who wrote the 'Foreword' to the Volume I here. I sent a copy of Volume I to Dr. Taylor who kindly wrote me back the aforecited letter that reveals his response about the Volume. He is no longer alive but I would remember him very much in my life.

This letter was an accolade to me. I did receive similar appreciation from a number of scholars from India and abroad. Professor W.G. Solheim II appreciated the Volume very much and so did Professor S.N. Rajaguru, Professor V.N. Misra, Dr. Eberhardt Fischer of Reitberg Museum, Zurich, Switzerland, Dr. Richard A. Engelhardt, UNESCO Regional Advisor for Culture in Asia and the Pacific, UNESCO Regional Office at Bangkok, Professor Mike Robinson, Department of Tourism and Cultural Change, Sheffield Hallam University, U.K., Dr. M. Taher, Dr. Birendranath Datta and many including my brother Late Surendra Nath Medhi. Professor V.N. Misra, former Director, Deccan College, Pune gave me his comment on the Volumes in his letter to me cited next,

"Dear Professor Medhi,

I have received copies of your two books and I am deeply thankful to you for sending the same to me. I have gone through the books and I give my brief comments below.

Northeast India, comprising Assam and six other states-Meghalaya, Arunachal Pradesh, Nagaland, Mizoram, Manipur and Tripura - is a fascinating land in may respects, its geology, geography, flora, fauna, and most particularly its people with their many languages, customs, music, dance, colourful costumes and ornaments. Unfortunately, the region is inadequately known to people outside it because of the lack of easy transport facilities like roads and railways, and also because there is a limited literature on it. The two publications by Professor Medhi and his colleagues, entitled Man and Environment in North East India, contribute greatly to filling this lacuna.

The first volume, an edited one, covers the topics geology, archaeology, ecology, man, society and language, similarities and differences among the tribal and non-tribal peoples of the region, traditional system of medicine and medicinal plants. The contributors are all well-known experts in their fields. Professor Medhi, the editor, himself is an internationally known scholar of archaeology, particularly ethnoarchaeology to the pursuit of which he has devoted several decades. The contributions are well written are very informative.

The second volume is a collection of articles of Professor Medhi written over last three decades or so. It covers a number of topics on both prehistoric and historic archaeology of the region, the Garos of Meghalaya, ethnoarchaeology, techniques of making stone tools and traditional system of medicine, etc. The articles, based on first hand fieldwork by Dr. Medhi, are marked by intimate knowledge of the author about the archaeology and people of the region.

The two volumes will contribute greatly to making the environment, archaeology and people of the north east region of the country better known to people outside the region both within the country and outside. Professor Medhi and his colleagues deserve our congratulations for bringing out these highly educative and important volumes.

V.N. Misra, 23.03.2004"

Today I remember Late Pradip Chaliha, a most dedicated researcher in the field of art, dance and culture of the region. Before his sad demise, I had long discussions with him regarding my introductory article in this Volume, and, he was kind enough to help me with lots of ideas, which I consider much useful. He was an authority on art, dance and culture and I am indeed grateful to him for his kind help and inspiration in the production of this Volume as 'Heritage Issue # 1'.

I would like to refer a photograph that was printed on the cover flap of Volume II. That was a picture I photographed at Bhoksong in Karbi Anglong district of Assam and depicted a composite picture of wet and *jhum* (Slash-n-burn) cultivations. This I mention here because there was no reference about the photograph in any part of Volume II. For this Volume, myself with our son- Dol with the kind assistance of Shri Dilip Changkakati composed a logo on the basis of Saint Sankardeva's *kala-kristi* (art and culture). The logo would appear as a registered emblem in all the forthcoming Volumes on 'Man and Environment In Northeast India' and heritage issues.

xiii

I am grateful to Dr. Richard A. Engelhardt, UNESCO Regional Advisor for Culture in Asia and the Pacific for kindly writing the 'Foreword' to the volume III.

Before I conclude, it will be appropriate to tell the contributors and reader of this volume which appears very late due to an indifferent attitude of Shri Ramesh Kumar and Shri Satish Kumar of M/S Omsons Publications, who started making this volume in 2003; but in 2007, Shri Satish informed me that its publication was not possible. Over telephone Shri Satish said, the volume was destroyed. It was unfortunate. Somehow, I managed to retrieve the mansuscript from my desktop at the initiative of EBH Publishers, Guwahati. I am indeed grateful to EBH for bringing out the volume.

Finally I am sincerely thankful to all the authors of the articles. I also remember all kinds of cooperation and help of my wife Anju and two sons- Pol and Dol. Shri Dhritiman Sarma, my Research Scholar, co-operated me in checking the proof; I am thankful to him.

Sorojini-Bharat
27 Professor's Colony
Guwahati 781 016: Assam

Dilip K. Medhi Ph.D.
Editor
Email: dkbharat1@sancharnet.in

INTRODUCING

HERITAGE CULTURE OF NORTHEAST INDIA

Dilip K. Medhi

One

Former Assam and the State of Tripura currently have a common territorial terminology – the *Northeast India*. It is more an administrative term, which neither conveys any meaning to the people and their colourful cultures of the region. Many overseas as well as Indian scholars are much skeptic about this terminology and ridicule it since the new name never carry any meaning to the people and the land of this interior territory situated between the mainland South Asia, the Southeast Asia and China. This author has given a new nomenclature to this landmass as the 'Great Indian Corridor in the East', in consideration with the importance of the region in respect of human migration between mainland the Southeast Asia and China together, and because of its major role in admixing the Indo-Aryan and the Mongoloid cultures.

Primarily aimed at throwing light on the heritage culture of Northeast India, the writer first makes an attempt to understand the meaning of heritage and consulted the New Webster Dictionary of the English language by Mario Pei who defines 'heritage' as "comes to or belongs to one by reason of birth; as, the *heritage* of longevity; a legacy, as of culture or tradition; something allotted to or reserve for one; as, the heritage of a title; law, that which may be inherited through the legal process, as property or land". Concerning the perimeters of this article, the writer adopts the term *heritage* that means, 'a legacy of culture or tradition'. The heritage is further divided into tangible and intangible ones. This in anthropology is understood as material and spiritual culture of man respectively. However it is the legacy, a culture or a tradition of human beings who develop it in a certain environment that suited them to live in. Henceforth a kind of ecological setting is developed, which tells about a man-plant relationship in an area of the planet earth.

Man is the only cultural animal of the Universe; he with his free hand and with an opposable thumb accompanied by a high brain capacity (1,650 cc) is capable of managing any kind of environment of the globe. Human being is so much technologically developed today compared to the remote past, can make anything possible including the production of human life with a most sophisticated technique of *cloning*. A discipline of genetic engineering is already in the hand of man, which made him capable of rectifying the erring genes in him. Dr. Hargobind Khorana, a scientist of Indian origin first made a synthetic **gene** and was awarded Nobel Prize in Medicine in 1968. But these are not the spontaneous and obvious behaviours of man since he requires highly sophisticated ability, and therefore not possible for man to inherit them in an ordinary way. Already the Governments of U.S.A. and U.K. have banned the human cloning and also a number of countries go against this piece of science. My son Darpan Kaustuv Medhi who is studying genetics and microbiology at the University of Sheffield, is optimistic of a great use of gene knowledge for rectification of erring gene of human being and thus in treatment of disease and ailments soon.

Human aptitude accompanied by an innate mental capability in a spontaneous way, can produce some kind of materials (tools or weapons) as well as non-material spiritual ideals for his subsistence, and, which as the life-style or as a prestigious means of life is adopted by his next generations. This life-style in course of time is termed as the heritage of a human community in a particular ecological setting of the world. Man universally made stone implements and the earthenware at different corners of the globe mostly without any kind of first hand communication between them; he made them automatically with a concerted effort followed by a kind of need. Here applies a popularly used statement, 'the psychic unity of mankind' propounded by Adolf Bastian (1826-1905), a 19th Century Polymath is best remembered for his contributions to the development of ethnography and the development of anthropology as a discipline; however the author would like to modify it to another form- 'the spiritual homogeneity of mankind' (www.en.wikipedia.org). According to Bastian, the contingencies of geographic location and historical background create different local elaborations of the "elementary ideas"; these he called "folk ideas" (*Volkergedanken*). Bastian also proposed a lawful "genetic principle" by which societies develop over the course of their history from exhibiting simple sociocultural institutions to becoming increasingly complex in their organization. The postulate of "the psychic unity of mankind" states that all human beings, regardless of culture or race, share the same basic psychological and cognitive make-up; we are all of the same kind. Adolf Bastian, the "father of German anthropology", who was a classical German humanist and a cultural relativist and one, who believed in the intrinsic value of cultural variation. Bastian passed it on to his similarly minded student, Franz Boas, who, as the "father of American anthropology", transmitted it on to all of his students. Edward B. Tylor introduced it to 19th century British evolutionist anthropology, where it became a fixture, defended by all the major British evolutionists. The postulate, indeed, was essential to the great comparative projects of evolutionism, which would be futile if cultural differences were determined by differing biology. For the same reason, it has been central to later compative projects, e.g. Radcliffe-Brown's, Barth's, Steward's, Godelier's and others. Today, the postulate is shared by all anthropologists, and this author too does excepting the wordings in the statement.

After man separated himself from the Primate, he began his terrestrial life at different situations with the strength of a common gene pool in him. Complexity that appeared in human being due to evlutionary processes also resulted in multiplication of genes in equal proportions. All sorts of development in an enviroment were scanned well in his vision. Matters were analysed in his mind, and they were all appropriately appropriated to benefit his adaptation. An appropriate matter was accordingly harnessed or systematised according to a kind of need i.e. for his subsistence. Emile Burns mentioned about matter and mind in his book 'What is Marxism'. Gordon Childe elaborately discussed on Social Evolution. Gene flow shall generate a common cerebral command resulting in production of same kind of tools, weapons including other material and spiritual matters as well. Therefore the author wants to modify the statement as stated above. To me Bastian's statement has strong psychological bias than ought to be anthropological. Nevertheless linkage of Anthropology with Psychology is undeniable. However in the opinion of this author, universally similar syndrome that appear in human being requires an exclusive anthropological interpretation.

E.B. Tylor and L.H. Morgan were the pioneers to work on human evolution particulalrly on human culture and of human society. Humankind irrespective of race, colour, caste and creed characterises a common physical make-up. Evolution physically advances man and did advance him in buillding cultural set-up from simple to complex in various environments. Handazes of Meghalaya and those found in South America look similar. Choppers made on huge pebbles at the foothills of Eastern Khasi Hills bordering Assam and discovered in December 2007 look similar to the Oldowan choppers, and if the entire December 2007discovery (choppers and other tools) is mixed with Oldowan tool assemblage, it would be very difficult to isolate them from the Oldowans.

Man at a number of great centres of Mesoamerica, Middle East and Southeast Asia made varieties of tools and produced different kind of foods through domestication of a wide variety of plants, animals and birds. These types of habits percolated from generation after generations and were identified later as an inseparable way of livelihood. With a dependable economy, man concentrated on a number of spiritual aspects of life like producing art form and to believing in the existence of souls; such kind of ideas afterward became a part of the day-to-day life of mankind. Finally man began to believe in some kind of supernatural powers, which they associated with varieties of natural disasters, and began to develop some contrivances to appease those powers. Many inanimate objects were later identified as the abode of divine powers and finally they become some kind of god to man who propitiated them and looked forward to receiving help and security from their survival. Consequently in course of time spiritual codes were framed in human society to worship supernatural power(s) or a god(s).

The writer likes to refer to E.B. Tylor who while giving a 'definition of culture' did include any kind of identifiable human traits and his mental capabilities acquired in a society of his kind. In 1874 Tylor in his classical definition on culture said, "Culture or civilization is that complex whole which include knowledge, beliefs, arts, morals, laws, customs and any other capabilities and habits acquired by man as a member of society". Therefore any kind of material expression of man and his spiritual ideas give rise to `human culture' that persists in the remote past and also continues to the present. They are manifested in mankind, which becomes the subject matter of heritage studies later.

Cultural traits of man remain trapped in an area of his habitation and also flourish if the occupancy continues in the same locality for a substantial occasion. However the migratory habit of man made to carry their cultural mannerism to different localities of the World; for example the cord-impressed pottery and the shouldered Celts are the two distinctive traits of the Neolithic culture in Southeast Asia, which are found to spread to Assam (currently Northeast India) with the migratory human progenies from the latter. Further the *sarâi* (a kind of plate with a stand made of cane and bamboo with its modern variety in bell metal and brass), which this writer could see in the Philippines, is also found extensively in the hills and plains of Assam. Therefore culture has a spatial and an itinerant dynamics as well. Traces of a culture in an area though look dead did never end in itself since nobody is certain enough about its dead characteristics and also about its proliferation during its existence. Illiot Smith (1911) was talking about the 'theory of diffusion' on the support of his studies in Egyptian cultures. Lewis R. Binford (1983) attempted to draw a connection between the past and the present though building of a 'middle range theory'. This writer asserted that 'present reflects the past', which tells about a cultural continuum in an area on the basis of supportive and collaborative traits of the present day surviving culture in that area (Medhi, 2002). It becomes a unique situation to draw a conclusion on continuity of culture via the 'middle range theory' or the theory of 'present reflects the past'. Nevertheless, situation arising out of a past static culture i.e. the ruins in an area without any living index to tell about its ongoing development or about its genesis, which however may be possible to draw with similar kind of ruins discovered elsewhere in relation to a contiguous culture of that area or away from it. A culture in continuity or a sporadic one is becoming subjects of research in archaeology under normal circumstances, and becomes special issues of research when they are considered as the heritage matter to a country and its civilization.

Having said about a *sarâi* that has much significance in the Assam region, another two items of heritage culture of the region include a g*amochâ* and a *jâpi*. *Gamochâ* with floral design is a prestigious towel produced in indigenous handlooms by the lady weavers of the region. *Jâpi,* is made of bamboo, cane and palm leaf, and the peasants use it on their heads as a traditional sunshade and a rainshade as well. This traditional sun-cum-rain umbrella with a little construction variation than those of Assam region is common in entire Southeast Asia and China. Today a *phulâm gâmochâ* (Assamese towel with blossom design and decoration) and a *phulâm jâpi* (a showpiece version of a sun-cum-rain umbrella with unique design and decoration) are high-status souvenirs of Assam presented while paying ovation to a distinguished guest or an eminent personality, and, people of the region keep them in the residential drawing rooms along with the *sarâi* of brass as ornamental pieces. These two items of Assamese heritage culture were first made popular to the common masses when *Rupknowar* Late Jyoti Prasad Agarwalla put them in the settings of *Joymati,* the first film in Assamese language produced in 1935 in this part of India.

Similar to the meaning and definition of a culture, 'heritage' may also be either 'a tangible one' or 'an intangible one'; tangible comprises the material evidence of a visible way of life whereas the intangible consists of spiritual aspect of traditions like music, arts and any other finer traits of mankind, which are reconstructed on the basis of certain evidence of culture- mostly material ones. Besides the material cultures of Neanderthal man, a number of finer achievements of them have been identified in respect of dress and food habits, man-to-man relationship, music and a belief in the existence of soul. That the Neanderthal man used a kind of dress in order to prevent them from the severe cold of Pleistocene times was evident from the side scrapers they made of stone and used to scrape out the flesh from the animal skin and trim it as well, which was used as a kind of earliest garment in the history of dress and ornaments of mankind. Analysis of coprolites tells about the use of meat in major proportion by them. Neanderthal man loved to sit closely and to cuddle each other's hair and head with fingertips and hand. They also produced a kind of music, may be to attract the animals to hunt. They put flowers on the dead body is an evidence of believing in 'soul'. All these traits referred to are the heritage of mankind, which flourished in different parts of the World independently or in contiguity with other cultures.

With this much of introduction to heritage culture of mankind in the light of its worldwide attributes in brief, the writer begins his journey in the present day Northeast India or the former Assam into the heritage culture of the region in the following.

The Assam Region or the Northeast India is an enchanting landmass with enormously beautiful hills and the plains inhabited by people with different sets of colourful cultures since the dim distant moment. The population is basically the tribals and the non-tribals; the former has an origin in Southeast Asia and China and the later in the mainland India. Before the advent of the Hinduism and later the Christianity, the tribal people were animist and believed in an animistic world with a number of supernatural powers those were believed to be bestowed in plants, animals and other inanimate objects like rock and hills. The tribals paid them great respect and propitiated them in their own way during certain parts of the year or when there appears a crisis in the society and to its members. Males of a particular community assemble together at a fixed place in their village where their supernatural power is believed to live in an organic or inorganic life form and propitiate the particular object with offerings of rice wine and sacrifice of fowls and pigs. Such kind of places is commonly seen in any tribal village of the Assam Region. Emergence of Hinduism with Aryan culture introduced a concept of worship to different gods and goddesses inside a cave, rock-shelter or a temple, and finally the propagation of *Neo-Vaishnavite* religion by great Saint Shri Shri Sankardeva resulted in the construction of *Nâmghar* and a *Sattra* complex where the devotees performed mass recital in the form of *nâm-prasnaga* to pray Lord Krishna. So among the Hindus too there exist different kinds of temple complex that acted as a platform for expression of their religious faiths. So from 3rd to 4th Century AD onward, the former Assam could see the construction of a number of temples and later from the 15th Century AD, *Nâmghar*s and *Sattra*s almost in every villages in the plains of Assam. Besides these tangible heritage in Assam Region, there are numerous intangible oral traditions in the form of music, dance, plays, devotional prayer, enchanting *mantra*s and Sanskrit *sloka*s which are intimately connected to those institutions including the animist societies of various religious traditions. Music and allied developments form the great oral masterpieces of mankind. In a trip to Lijiang, P. R. China, the writer and his wife attended two great sessions of 22 hundred years' old *Naxi* Music of South China, and could see the participation of a number of artists in the age-group of 90 years+. This type of situations, I am afraid although available, but definitely not older like that of the *Naxi* Music in this part of India, is gone unnoticed and untapped. However Assam has more than 500 years old *Sâttriya* music and dance Saint Shri Shri Sankardeva created and developed in the 15th Century AD. *Manipuri* dance is another form of national dances of *Manipur* that was developed in 17th Century AD. Both the *Sattriyâ* dances and music and also the Manipuri dance are recognized form of National classical dance and music of India.

The temple of *Mâ Kâmâkshyâ* or *Mâ Kâmâkhyâ* at the Nilachal Hill, Guwahati is one of the oldest places of pilgrimage in Indian Subcontinent. It is considered as the great *Yoni Pith* of mother goddess. Lady Parvati represents the goddess of *Shakti* in Hindu mythology. *Brahmakunda* near Sadiya in Upper Assam is another holy place of the Subcontinent. Lord *Parsurâm,* one of the 10th incarnations of *Vishnu* in his endeavour to make himself free from heinous peccadillo of killing his mother, scotfreed the course of the River Brahmaputra from a gorge called the *Brahmakunda*. They, the *Kâmâkshyâ* temple and the *Brahmakunda* or *Parsurâmkunda* attracted plenty of visitor-devotees from different parts of mainland India since the days of early historic times. Devotees have great reverence in them as the important places of pilgrimage and assemble there at different esteemed occasions- during *Ambubâsi melâ* in June 22-25 to *Kâmâkshyâ* and at the time of *Makar Sakrânti* at middle of January to *Brahmakunda* every year. *Kâmâkshyâ* was reached through the *Purba Sâgar* (Eastern Sea) and via the

River Brahmaputra; devotees arrived at *Brahmakunda* via a land route on the north bank of Brahmaputra or may be partly by river and partly by the land route. Assam region has innumerable river network and the river transport served as a major transportation system in this part of India and it connected most of the temples and holy places of the region.

The great Indian epic *Mahâbhârata* mentions about the participation of the *Kâmarupi* Raja (King of Kâmarupa State) Bhagadatta who joined the battle of Kurukshetra in support of his son-in-law Duryodhana, the eldest Kaurava. While taking part in the war, Bhagadatta led a major attachment of elephants with huge contingent of soldiers. It is a known fact that the Assam region is rich in feral elephants and elephant catching through *melâ-shikar,* a traditional practice of catching wild elephant was a major event in this part of India. Wild elephant were later tamed by local *mâhuts* for commercial uses. Assam has a famous lady Ms. Parbati Baruah from Gauripur, Goalpara, who earned her name well as the only lady trainer or *mahut* of wild elephant. Mention about the white elephant (albino variety) comes from the literary evidence particularly from *Hastividârnava* composed during the Ahom Kingdom at the patronage of Ahom King Shiva Singha and his queen Ambika Devi.

The former Assam has a past record of receiving visitors of World fame, and they were Marco Polo, three Chinese travelers- Fahien (5th Century AD), Hiuensang (630 AD) and I-tsing (700 AD) and also a record of two pilgrimage routes mentioned earlier, one through surface on the northern bank of the River Brahmaputra up to *Parsurâm Kunda* and another by *Purba Sâgar,* a sea of that time to visit *Kâmâkshyâ* temple of *Kâmarupa;* however they were completed partly via River Brahmaputra and the land route as well. Today the land route is represented by the former *Gohâi Kamal Ali* of Ahom age. In textbook of Geology, existence of a sea called *Tethys* in the present day territories of West Bengal and Bangladesh is recorded and, *Tethys* might represent the *Purba Sagar* that touches *Kâmarupa*. Formerly the territories of Bengal were non-existent in the map of ancient India and it had no record in Indian epics, and the former Assam was directly connected to mainland India through those routes. In addition to those two routes, the Chinese travelers visited this part of India from Yunnan through Tirap frontier of present day Arunachal Pradesh, which is already termed as one of the famous *silk routes.* The other *silk route* was via central Asia through the Gobi desert and passing through the Pamir plateau reaching the Western Asia. There were more distinguished visitors who wrote about ancient Assam, and they were Damodargupta who traveled with Joypiba Lalitaditya (son of Lalitaditya who married Amritprabha of Assam) and later wrote *Kuttiniyattam* (755-786 AD), Minhajuddin who wrote Tabakat-e-Nachiri after traveling with General Bakhtiar Khiliji (13th Century AD), Captain Wales (18th Century AD) who came to subjugate the *Moamoriâ* rebels in Assam during the reign of King Gaurinath Singha, Sahabuddin Talish with General Mirjumla (January 4, 1662 to January 9, 1663) and Shouan-Shoyan (7th Century AD) during King Bhaskar Varma's rule in *Kâmarupa*. Ptolemy in addition to the different notes on Assam wrote eloquently about the region from secondary sources.

The region has a famous indigenous silk industry that made wide ranging varieties of dresses during the Ahom rule, particularly for its kings, queens and the ministers besides its current all India and overseas reputations. Assam's golden silk, a unique and exclusive to the region is famous World over. Noteworthy to mention is Assam had a *silk route* with China in the past. The former territories of Assam that shared a long international boundary with China had indeed a good relation with the latter. North Eastern Frontier Agency or NEFA, currently called the Arunachal Pradesh situates close to Tibet and the southern provinces of China. Assam and China have almost an equal status in respect of the silk production. Women of Assam region very well nurture the silkworm and the *endiworm* in their houses; moreover State Sericulture Departments also largely cultivate them. At present China brings up large-sized silkworms, which almost double the size of the Assamese ones. Apart from two varieties of silk, *endi,* a warm cloth of Assam and, which every Assamese people own. The women folk further produce finest cotton textile in their indigenous handlooms. It is claimed that cloths produced by the Assamese weavers was of superb quality and could be desiccated in shade, and also could be held in a handgrip due to its finest textural excellence. Both tribal and the non-tribal populations of the region are equally adept in handloom profession over various kinds of handlooms available at different parts of the region. Womenfolk master the art of manufacturing varieties of dye with indigenous ingredients from local herbs and minerals. Women proficiently used alkali and alcohol bases to make a dye much durable and permanent. The tradition of making colourful dresses continues and its record comes from the *Vaishnavite* religious traditions when Shri Shri Sankaradev made a celebrated 60-yard long *brindâvani bastra* where His Holiness depicted the *pât of sât Vaikuntha.* It was produced at Tâtikuchi (present day Barpeta) and is currently preserved at the British Museum, United Kingdom.

Besides the expertise in the field of indigenous textile, women of Assam region equally mastered the storage know-how of cloths. Silk garments are a prestigious pastime of the ladies of the region. Women produce and use a wide range of colourful dresses, and take enormous care to preserve them in their indigenous containers. Silk fabrics were preserved inside earthen pots- *debitâ* or *dâabâr* and those of cotton yarns either in *petâry* made of cane or in *perâ* made of bamboo. Potters of this region made large earthenware, mostly huge jars for such purposes. *Petâry* and *perâ* are two large varieties of storage bins with lids. While putting the cloths inside them, dry *neem* leaves as good in lieu of modern insecticide were put inside to prevent the cloth from the attack of vermin. This system of storage of clothing still continues in rural areas; however with the advent of the iron storage facilities during the British rules, such practices began to disappear in the urban localities with affluent families.

In the coming few lines the writer likes to describe the toiletry and luxuries connected to the beauties of women in this part of India. Beauty of an Assamese damsel makes a synthesis of the Mongoloid and the Aryan characters; their faces are mostly oval with high up cheeks and skin colour is fair. Plain (leiotrichy) black hair of sizeable length similar to those of Mediterranean region makes the ladies more charming and beautiful too. Consumption of fish protein in plenty is considered the primary factor behind the story of the beautiful long black hair. Fish protein and also the sour vegetables naturally make the skin colour flabbier.

Hardworking ladies in agrarian economy of Assam could barely attend to their toiletry and luxuries in an elaborate way excepting on a festive and other need based occasions like marriage ceremonies. Leaf, flower, stem and root ingredients contribute in this feminine pastime. Initially people of Assam particularly the ladies did use the sesame oil with additive fragments of *gondh birinâ* (Lemon grass; *Cymbopogon*) on hair to make their hair more blackish, shining and sweet-smelling. This oil was kept in wooden or bamboo container with an additive ingredient for fragrance.There is a popular saying, *Hajor Natir Kibâ Kâm, Telor Târi Phani Khân*. Hajo is a famous pilgrim in Assam that embraces the Hindu, Buddhism and Islam religions. Hajo is a 'Panchatirtha' in Assam. *Devadâsi* or temple dancers of Hajo at its *Mâdhab-Kedâr Mandir* were well known in entire Assam. This saying is related to Hajo *Devadâsis*, which states that the *Devadâsis* (*Nati*) of Hajo were always busy in dressing their hair meaning oiling their hair and comb i.e. coiffure it always. While it is an obvious practice of a *Nati* at Hajo, the Assamese woman combed their hair after oiling at post-mid day meal as well as at night before going to bed. Assamese ladies use locally extracted sesame and mastered oils for massaging (*tel sonâ*) hairs. While shampooing hair, inner contents of a *ghilâ* (Entada: *Entada scandens*) , foliage leaf of sesame plant, paste of *âkâshi latâ (Cuscuta reflexa Roxb.)* and mastered oil cakes were in weekly use. To make the black hair more shining, hair was treated with paste of black gram mixed with mastered oil. This treatment not only made the hair further black, but also equally helped in making the brown and silky hair more blackish. Pradip Chaliha who did considerable research on heritage culture of undivided Assam said, he was having brown hair while he was a young boy, and his friends often laughed at him when he was living in Sylhet of Bangladesh with his parents before pre-Independence India. Finally at the advice of a senior lady he made his hair black with the use of a paste of black gram and mustard oil (Personal communication, 2003). Paste of *Jetukâ* leaf (Henna plant) and betel leaf was another herbal mixture that was equally used for a similar purpose. Paste of *silikhâ (Terminalia citrina)* and *âmlokhi* (Emblic) was another device of treating the hair of female. Facial beautification and treatment was mostly made with mustard oil; however wash with tepid *Neem* water (water boiled with *Neem* leaf) was a major use besides occasional bath with Neem water was another way of treatment of skin. *Neem* water was further used in treatment of skin of a person after he/she has some kind of skin disease or may be after an attack by missals or chicken pox. Moreover Assamese ladies put on paste of turmeric, raw tealeaf, pilfer of orange and *Neem* stem in their facial treatment. Although knowledge about body perfume is much limited, pulp of sandalwood was definitely used for enhancing the body and facial beauty equally, and for fragrance as well. *Agar* plant grew plenty in this part of India and if the *agar* extract was made available for such purposes is not known. Scented herbs like *gondh birinâ* was in use as an additive to make the hair oil fragranced. *Keteki* (*Pandanus tectorius Soland.*) is a famous plant of attractive fragrance and was used with a few finger strokes at the two sides of the forehead and in fact, pollens of *keteki* brings the much attractive smell. Moreover flowers like *juti* (mogra), *kharikâjâi* and *tagar* were wonderful either to be put in water for bath or a facial wash as well, besides sometimes putting them in drinking water.

Assamese dress and ornaments are rated as one of the finest in the Indian Subcontinent and World over as well. Mention has been made about the quality of the Assamese fabric earlier. Ladies use a piece of *mekhelâ*, a *châddar*, a *rihâ* and a blouse as the national dress. However use of a blouse was confined with the royal and the aristocrats, and was never used by the common Assamese ladies before the British regime in India. Normally a lady in rural Assam uses a *mekhelâ* and a *châddar* with a veil. Dresses are made from both the cotton and silk yarn. Ornaments were of gold and silver. Assamese woman has varieties of ornaments that they wear on head, nose, ear, neck, wrist, arm, waist and at the ankle, and, every piece of them has different names. A *jethi* which is called *chitipati* in Bengali is either a single or trident chain placed over the head of a lady and much particularly of a bride. A *jethi* having a single chain goes through the central furrow of head hair and the trident with three chains goes over the sides of the head besides one goes through the central hair furrow. Nose was adorned with varieties of *nâk-phool made* of either gold or silver studded with precious, semi-precious or fancy stones. *Kânphool, kerumoni, jâpi, lokâpâra, sonâ, kadam, jijiri kadam, thuriâ or keru, bâli or kân-bâli* and *kundal either a makar kundal or a karna singha* are some of the names of the different range of ear ornaments those vary from light to heavy in weight. Neck of an Assamese woman is adorned with a number of necklaces that are known as *galpâtâ, prajâpati hâr, jonebiri, benâ, dugdugi, shripad, moni, mâduli, dhol, charatiâ*, and *lokâpâra* may be exclusively on gold or with a combination of gold and beads of precious/semi-precious stones. Other may be made of beads and gold, gold studded with precious, semi precious or fancy stones. *Khâru* is a common word of wristlet (bangle). *Khâru* is either made on gold or silver and is equivalent to the size of a glass *churi*, a popular wrist ornament of ladies in the Indian Subcontinent. Assam has *gâmkhâru, muthikhâru* and *dhansirikhâru*- all massive bangles made of gold or silver and measures 6-7 Cms in length. *Gâmkharu* is a prized item of a wealthy lady and so also with the royal families and landlords. Precious stones are also embedded in them. A similar type of ornament is used at the upper arm and called the *baju*; and it may be a spiral bar of gold or silver. A golden or a silver chain at the waist made a thin waist of a lady more gorgeous. It has elaborate design and is called the *kardhani* or a *chandrahar* or a *mekhalâ, kingkini* and *katisutra* are its Sanskrit equivalents. *Bhor-khâru, bhori-khâru* or a *chele-khâru* is mostly a silver anklelet with ringers the Assamese ladies wear around their feet. A mother makes her child to wear it to detecting the child's movement. In Assam region gold was extracted from the silt of the Brahmaputra River and also at *Sowansiri* River, a tributary of the former. Finally an Assamese lady wearing a gorgeous silk dress along with all kinds of ornaments in her body and with a gorgeous hair knot gives her a magnificent heritage status. Moreover a blotch of vermilion at her forehead and also at the furrow of her head hair, and with the said fashion in case of a Hindu woman brings her more splendid look.

The woman of Assam region is well known for their magnificent hairstyle similar to those of the mainland Indian woman, and in fact, they love to dress their meticulously maintained long hair everyday. Enormously long hair could be seen in this part of India as a part of a prime beauty of a lady and such a bunch of hair grow beyond their knee-joints. To arrange a lady's hair in the form of a braid ranging from one to three pieces is a common practice in case of an unmarried damsel; these may be later put into a knot (*khopâ*), which is called the *chele-khopâ* or *chela-khopâ*. Knot or a *khopâ* is a significant hair pastime of the married woman, and specially to a bride.

A *khopâ* has varieties of category besides the 1. the *chele-khopä* or *chela-khopâ*. They are, 2. *Koldiliâ khopâ* resembles a banana blossom; 3. *Negheri-khopâ*, an especially stylistic hair-knot the *Devadâsi* at *Negheriting Dol* near Dergaon proficiently made in the past. It is also known as the *Udhaniâ-khopa* (similar to the *Udhan* or an earthen fire-pillar in rural Assam), *Ucchal-khopâ* and *Natini-khopâ* (the hair-knot of a *Nati* or *Devadasi* or a temple dancer in a temple of Assam). These two hair-knots are strikingly tall ones. 4. *Ghilâ-khopâ* meaning another hair-knot the woman makes like the seed of Entada. 5. *Ligiri-khopâ is* a quick hairstyle proviso the *ligiri*s or maidservants made at a royal palace or at a landlord's place. *Ligiri-khopâ* was a tight hair-knot since the maidservant has to work at the palace like spindle and, therefore, hairstyle of the maidservants must never be deceptive at any moment. 6. *Doluâ-khopâ* is a compact hair-knot that a woman makes in their day-to-day life. 7. A *Kâcheri-khopâ* or a *Kachri-khopâ* is another style in hair-knots and is connected with the *Deodhâni* culture of tribals, and a *deodhâni* lady makes this knot while she dances in sitting posture before the altar. 8. *Kanâri-khopâ* is a not an indigenous hairstyle of the region. It is often found amongst the tea garden labour communities in Assam, who were brought from Kanara areas of mainland India. Specialty in this hair-knot, the hairs is tied on one side of the head.   This is a common hair fashion found with the tribals living in the Chotanagpur plateau. Moreover in Assamese literature including the *Harmohan Upakhyan* in *Kirttan-Ghosâ* composed by Guru Shri Shri Sankardeva referred about the *Ucchal-khopâ*, an elaborative hairstyles of Assamese lady while narrating the wonderful beauty of a woman. Sometimes a beautiful lady makes a fabulous but loose hair knot with an inherent tendency to make a show of her sparkling long and massive bunch of hair together with her grandiose beauty in a voluptuous '*hansa-gâmini* foot step' meaning the stylistic footstep of a swan. Woman of Assam region are well versed with the art of maintenance of beauty, and could make grandiose appearance with beautiful dresses and ornaments together with emphatic hairstyle and with or without a vermilion spot on her forehead. Their gorgeous appearance becomes much attractive with beautiful dress and ornaments at the Bihu festivals, on the occasion of marriage ceremonies and other festivals of Assam region. Moreover they like to dress themselves beautifully at the time of paying social visits.

While describing the heritage dress and ornaments of an Assamese lady, the innumerable tribals of Northeast India have their individual dresses and ornaments and they are used on an occasion of their festivals. The Jaintia ladies of Meghalaya wear heritage apparel at the time of the *Nokrem* dance, which is held at Smit in Upper Shillong every year. It is a most prestigious dance of the Jaintias, and the King of Jaintias at Smit in Upper Shillong annually organizes the *Nokrem* dance festival at the premises of his traditional royal palace. The Garo woman has their own heritage attire with plenty of bead necklaces that cover almost two-third of the chest from neck to the waist and a kind of black dress. Garo damsels also wear colourful quill on their heads besides a cloth turban at the time of *Wangala* festival, the high-status national dance form of the Garos.

To be continued ....

References:

Binford Lewis R.1983 *In Pursuit of the Past.* London and New York: Thames and Hudson.

Medhi Dilip K. 2002 Ethnoarchaeology in Northeast India. *Man and Environment in Northeast India, Vol. II: 10-27.* New Delhi: Omsons Publications.

Smith Eliot Grafton. 1911 *The Ancient Egyptians.* London: Mcmillan.

Tylor Edward Burnett.1874 *Primitive Culture* (2 Volumes: 1st American & 2nd English Edition). New York.

www.en.wikipedia.org/adolf_bastian

SHRI SHRI SANKARADEVA AND HIS CONTRIBUTION TO CULTURE AND CIVILIZATION OF INDIA

Maheswar Neog

In August-September 1449 Sankardeva was born in a Kayastha family in village Bardowa on the southern bank of River Brahmaputra in the present-day district of Nagaon, Assam. His father, Kusumavara was the *Siromani* or overlord of a number of chiefs or landlords known as *Bhuyan*s, who ruled over principalities of varying sizes lying on both the banks of the River Brahmaputra. He was, as popularly believed, the fruit of a boon obtained from Lord Siva enshrined in a nearby temple, and came to be known on that account as Sankara or Sankaravara. He lost his mother, Satyasandhya, soon after his birth and his father left him to the loving care of his grandmother Khersuti. Sankara grew up to a well-built and lovely lad. But his boyish pranks knew no bounds. He loved ever to live an open air life, going after the cattle, swimming across the strong currents of the mighty Brahmaputra, wrestling with his play-mates and playing all the time. He was twelve years of age, but had no mind to go to school. One day his grandmother took advantage of his sitting to a heavy meal to remind him how scholarly were his forefathers and how he made a sad contrast by proving himself to be no better than a street urchin even at the age of twelve! Sankara was cut the quick. He submitted himself to the control of his grandmother, who took him to a renowned *pandit* Mahendra Kandali and put him into Kandali's boarding school. But he found the hard work at studies very irksome and tried to steal a day's holiday by bribing the *pandit* with a little money and a piece of cloth. Kandali, however, reported the whole matter to Sankara's grandmother,who scolded the grandchild very severely indeed. The reprimand had the desired effect, for Sankara spared no pains to pore over ancient folios. He achieved miracles by becoming a scholar in the conventional Sanskrit lore in about six years, by being able to compose a hymn in the tripping *totaka* metr(rhyme without vowel symbol) at the beginning of his student career, and by writing in verse a narrative, *Harischandra-upakhyâna,* when still at school. He paid his *guru* handsomely for the education he got and returned to his family.

Sankara's relatives insisted on his taking up the duties of *Siromani Bhuyan,* whereas he himself preferred a life of scholastic and religious persuasion. Under the kinsfolk's pressure he was forced to marry at the age of twenty-one. He was also installed as *Siromani.* All the same, he did not give up his scholarly habits. About four years after the marriage a daughter was born that was followed soon by the death of Sankara's wife, which made him lose all interest in worldly life. He waited till the sixth or seventh year of his daughter so that she might be married to an able *Kayastha* youth.This done he assigned the over-lordship to two of his uncles and set out on his first pilgrimage at the age of thirty-two years in 1481 AD in the company of seventeen others, including his teacher, Mahendra Kandali, and his lifelong friend and associate. Ramarama Vipra. He visited Puri, Gaya, Prayaga, Vrindavana, Mathura, Kurukshetra and other holy places. It is not certain whether he traveled in Southern India as some later biographers would like us to believe. It was at Badarikashrama that he made one of his earliest lyrics (*bargita*) beginning

Rest my mind, rest on the feet of Rama, Seest thou not the great and approaching ?

My mind, every moment life is shortening, just heed, any moment it might fleet off.

It is clear that a sense of transitoriness of life and the world had seized the mind of this young man very strongly. Although he remained away from home for twelve years, it is probable that he spent a considerable part of this long time in Puri. Born a *Sakta*, he seems to have a revelation there and to have come to the firm faith that devotion to one god. Lord Krishna or *Jagannatha*, alone could lead men to Supreme Bliss. He had no spiritual preceptor and *Jagannatha* is considered to have taken place in his life.

When Sankara returned home in 1493 AD his mind was charged with the warmth of a new faith of Love, *bhakti dharma*. He saw how the holy places like Puri and Varanasi were echoing with a new type of songs. Fain would he now devote all his energies to the propagation of his *dharma*. His kinshfolk took note of this and pressed on him to marry again and resumed the duties of *Bar-Bhuyan* or *Siromani Bhuyan.* He yielded on the first point and married Kalindi, but, declining to be an administrator again. Had a temple built for him so that he could sit with other people to discuss matters spiritual and hold prayers. A Tirhut Brahmin, Jagadisa Misra, brought him from Puri the full text of the *Bhagavata-Purana,*furnished with Sridhara Swami's *Bhavartha-dipika* commentary. He went deep into this *bhakti* text as interpreted by one of its best commentators, and seriously started on the programme of proselytizing and building a literature in the Assamese language to incorporate the soul of *bhakti*. Thus he composed some sections of his most popular work. '*Kirtana-ghosha'* narrating tales from the *Bhagavata-purana* and other holy texts. In these he propounded the doctrines of his *ekasarana nâma dharma,* enjoining unswerving devotion to one god, Vishnu-Krishna and, prayers as the sole *sâdhana* of that devotion.

It is about this time that Sankaradeva is believed to have organized a dramatic performance, *Chihna-yâtrâ,* depicting Vishnu in his celestial abode in a series of seven scenes painted as background on paper. For this he had to make very elaborate preparations by having *mridangas* and other instruments made for him and rehearsing the actors and musicians. He himself played the role of Narayana at one stage and charmed the theatre-goers with marvelous dances. A great number of people were attracted to him, and he now became a preacher, receiving his teacher, Mahendra Kandali, and his class-mate and family priest Ramarama Vipra, among the first neophytes.

The Bhuyan's territories bordered on the lands held by the Tibeto-Burman tribe, Kacharis, who started creating troubles for these chiefs leading to skirmishes between the two groups. Sankaradeva, who wanted a quiet life for his spiritual activitides, migrated with all the Bhuyans to the northern bank of the Brahmaputra and settled finally at a place, Gangamau, near modern Biswanathghat. But the Coches under the leadership of Visvasimha were establishing a Kingdom with Coch-Behar as its centre, and the Bhuyans in Kamarupa were already feeling the impact of Visvasimha's expansionism. Seeing this, Sankaradeva and his company of Bhuyans moved once again to the east and, entering the Ahom Kingdom made their abode in the River Island of Majuli at a place called *Dhuwâhât* or Beloguri. *Dhuwâhât* has its derivative from the word *'Bhuyâhât'*, which was a commercial centre or *hât* populated by Bhuyâns. It was here, on one hand, that Sankaradeva, acquired the companionship of a brilliant Kayastha youth, Madhavadeva, later to be his closest disciple and finest apostle, after a very keen debate, for the latter was till then a staunch Sâkta, believing that the primordial power of the world in the form of a goddess has to be propitiated with many animal sacrifices and, on the other hand, he had a stiff confrontation with the *tântrics* and scholars belonging to various shades of Indian thought. Some of his protagonists of heterodox faiths abused the ears of the Ahom monarch of the land with foul reports about his missionary activities. The Saint was summoned to the capital for a trial, but had an honourable acquittal when facts about his faith and philosophy were made known to the King. Nothing daunted, the adversaries tried another trick and raised fears of subversion in the King's mind.The Bhuyans of Dhuwahat were called to an elephant-catching *kheddâ* operation but, not being used to it, let the elephants escape through the areas of their vigilance. The King ordered arrest of the principal Bhuyans. Sankaradeva somehow escaped, but his son-in-law Hari together with Madhavadeva were taken in chains to the capital, Gargaon. The son-in-law was put to the executioner's sword and Madhavadeva, apparently saintly, was detained there for six months. This greatly embittered the Saint's feelings, who on Madhava's return decided to go to the Coch Kingdom, because the new King, Naranarayana, and his brother and commander-in-chief of the army, Chilaraya, were known to have a love of learning and piety.

Naranarayana and Chilaraya led an inroad into the Ahom Kingdom in 1546 AD and advanced as far as Narayanpur at a small distance from Dhuwahat. Sankaradeva and others took advantage of this and with the help of some Vhuyans (Bhuyans) already in the Coch camp sailed down the Brahmaputra in a number of boats. They entered Kâmarupa and after staying in several places settled at Barpeta. His life in the Coch State was of comparative quiet. But even here the old priesthood offered hostility to his creed and tried to win over the King against his church. On the other hand, he acquired a great number of disciples here, and it was to his advantage that Chilaraya married the daughter of his cousin, Ramaraya. Some good people like Narayana Thakura, and others joined the order of Sankaradeva.

About 1550 AD Sankaradeva took 120 disciples and set out on a second pilgrimage to Puri, coming back home after some six months. An old man now, he devoted his time to holding congregations, receiving neophytes and writing books. Among the new converts the notable were Ananta Kandali, a Brahmin scholar and poet, the chief of Heremda, and a Muslim, Chandcai. The activities of the *Vaishnava* fraternity increased to such a degree as to cause disquiet in the old priestly circles, which started a campaign of vilification in the capital and elsewhere. Naranarayana was much infuriated to hear exaggerated and distorted reports about the Saint's doings, and sent some sentries to bring down the social rebel in chains. The saint could not be apprehended. Two of his followers, Narayana Thakura and Gokulachanda, were dragged from Barpeta to Coch Behar and put to the severest forms of torture in an attempt to extort news about the Master. The two Vaishnavas refused to divulge anything and were, therefore, sold to some Bhutanese traders, who, however, were impressed by their devoutness and released them.The two sentries who carried Narayana and Gokulchanda back to the capital became ready converts to the new faith.

The King sent his men a second time to bind down Sankaradeva. Chilaraya, however, sensed his brother's fury and sent his own men to take his uncle-in-law safe to his own quarters. When Naranarayana pressed on Chilaraya to hand over the religious rebel to him, the latter obtained the assurance from the King that no injury would be done to the person of the Saint before the trial was over. Sankaradeva accordingly presented himself at the Coch royal court. His genial personality, his poetical and philosophical disposition coming out in the measure of a few Sanskrit and Assamese verses of his own composition, which he recited with his deep and mellifluent voice, and in the form of the discourse that immediately followed, made a very deep impression on the King, who had his early education in Varanasi. Day in and day out, there was a series of religious disputation with the Brahmin scholars of the land who for the most held *tântric* views, and each day brought signal triumph for the Vaishnava saint. The result was that Naranarayana became a friend to the Saint and remained so till the last and that Sankaradeva had often to shuttle between his temple *(Sattra)* at Patbausi (Barpeta) and Coch Behar. He often stayed with Chilaraya, who built him a temple at Bhela in the capital itself, and inspired him to have a forty-yard-long piece of cloth woven to depict Krishna's life in Vrindavana in colours and to write a drama, *Rama-Vijaya,* and produced it with his (Chilaraya's) actors (*nartaka*s). This piece of writing is dated l490 *saka* (1568 AD).

Within a few months of its production the Master passed away on the 7th or 21st Bhadra of the same *Saka* year and was given a state funeral on the banks of the small River, *Torocha.*

Sankaradeva was primarily a religious leader and reformer. He found Assam disunited through many creeds and forms.There was no peace in the land as it was divided politically. He himself belonged to the ruling Bhuyan Community, which held various principalities spotting the plains from the northeastern corner of the modern Coch Behar. The different tribes held their own in different places, particularly in the hills and in the backwoods. Of the different religions prevalent in the land, Saktism was the strongest and it got mixed up with debased forms of Buddhist *tântricism* to create a turbid atmosphere. The *Kâlikâ Purâna*, a 'left-hand' text, ordained *pancamakara,* the *Sabarotsava* reeking of frank sensuality, a great variety of blood sacrifices, virgin worship, and other peculiar forms. Some of these extreme rituals were carried on fearlessly in the main centers of *Saktism* like Nilachala (Kâmâkshyâ temple) and Sadiya (Tamresvari temple). The sacrifice of animals in their hundreds was revolting to Sankaradeva and some of his followers, and they declared themselves strongly against it. In order to get rid of other unhappy associations of *tantricism*, they described the worship of *Sakti, Siva* and other deities whatsoever. In the words of Dr. S.K. Chatterji (1970), "Sankaradeva was successful in applying the salve of religion to a people distracted in mind and body and brought to them spiritual peace and contentment and helped them on their way to having a better organized life". Fortunately for the people the Ahom power, established in the eastern region early in the 13th Century, expanded westward, and the 16th Century saw the rise and expansion of the Coch power further west so that the small principalities of Bhuyans and others were subjugated, thus leading to a balance of power between the Ahoms and Coches so that a new Assamese culture, as was evolved by Sankaradeva, could emerge as a cementing principle over Northeastern India with its predominantly Mongoloid population.

The particular form of *Vaishnavism* evolved by Sankaradeva is known as *ekasarana namadharma* (religion of prayers with the ultimate refuge in one God). It enjoined the worship of one God, that is, Vishnu in his many incarnations, chiefly as Krishna and Rama, and interdicted its votaries from the worship of any other deity, because as the *Bhâgavata-purâna* urges, it is enough to water the roots of a tree by which the branches and foliage get their sap or give food to the *pranas* by which limbs get their nourishment. Or, as the *Bhâgavadgitâ* demands, one should take sole refuge in the Bhâgavat, the Powerful Lord, who saves one from the faults of omission of all other duties, *bhakti* included in its fold eight different forms of *kirtana* (recital of praises to the Lord), *sravana* (listening to the praise of the Lord), *archana* or *puja* (worship to an idol with flowers and other offerings), and so on. But Sankaradeva declared *kirtana* and *sravana* to be the main forms out of these eight, and that is why his religion is called *sravana-kirtana-dharma* or *nâma-dharma.* Then again, it is popularly known as *Mahâpurushiyâ dharma,* because its worship is of the *mahâpurusha (parama-purusha or purushottama)*, the Supreme person, who lords over Primal *Prakriti* and *Purusha,* the procreators of the world of being. The holy services in the temples (known as *Sattra)* are known as *Hariprasanga* or *Nâma-prasanga* and these are mostly congregational prayer in songs, recitations, expositions of *Sâstras* and, sometimes dramatic pieces. These could be attended by all men (not women though) irrespective of caste distinctions and could be conducted by persons not ranked according to caste. The religious preceptor could also be of a lower social order than the disciple. Thus a sort of social equality was achieved even though the caste order was not done away with.

Sankaradeva and his chief apostle Madhavadeva composed a large literature, which provides the canonical basis as well as materials for the daily and seasonal temple services. There are songs like *ghosâ* (containing a couplet) *bargita* (a type of song tuned to different melody-modes at par Indian classical *râga*s), *bhatimâ* (eulogistic song), and *kirtana-ghoshâ* (sometimes forming part of a long narrative). In some of Sankardeva's books like *Harichandra-upakhyana, Amrita-manthana* and *Balichalana,* stories from the *Bhagavata-purâna* and Vaishnavite tales from other *Purânas* are retold in simple verses. Sometimes again, the Saint follows the original *Bhâgavata* in making a sequence of verses, which may not conform to the set standard of a *khanda-kâvya* or narrative. In *Bhakti-pradipa* and *Niminava-siddha-samvada,* he expounds the principles of *bhakti.* His Sanskrit treatise, *Bhaktiratnakara*, on the same themes covers a large field and draws from various *Purânas,* works like *Bhâgavadgitâ* and authors like Sankara the Advaitin, Krishna Misra Yati and Silhana Misra. He has six dramas that include *Rukmini-harana, Parijata-harana* and others, the tradition of the production of which still continues in some *Sattras* in its glory. These dramas contain in them a number of well-made Sanskrit verses and a number of songs (*ankiya gita* and bhatimâ) in an artificial idiom created by him for the plays and the *bargitas*. His writings still reign supreme among devout people, and his songs are ever on their lips.

Sankaradeva bequeathed a very rich legacy of classical tradition in music and dancing to his people. His dance-dramas make a community with such heritages as *bhagavata-melâ* and *Yakshagana* of the South and *Rama Lila* and *Rasa Lila* of the North. Much of this tradition has withered away for want of proper culture, but a good deal of its beauty still persists. The Vaishnava culture of Assam also nurtured the growth of a school of painting in Assam.

The philosophical basis of Sankaradeva's Vaishnavism is *Vedântic*. His *Vedântic* views have a large monistic bias thus making up a peculiar religious mysticism.

To conclude, I (1955:121-122) would like to quote from my work : "Sankaradeva's benign influence has been felt for the last few Centuries in all fields of the cultural life of the Assamese people. Thousands of devotees still visualize to themselves every day the physical beauty of the Master in its resplendent and almost transcendent glory, as has been painted by his dearest follower, Madhava.

Equal to Sankara's physical strength and beauty was his intellectual stamina and excellence. A versatile genius, he combined in himself many wonderful qualities. He was an administrator (as a *Siromoni Bhuyan*) and later a *gomâstâ* under Coch regime and social reformer, poet and dramatist, painter, musician and actor in dance-dramas. Wide and deep was his reading, and firm and persistent his intellectual grasp. In religious disputations he pushed his antagonists with sincere and persuasive arguments to the defeated corner. He often worked up the citations put forward by the opponents to his own advantage and made them move of themselves to his conclusions. His organizing capacity manifested itself in the way he placed the doctrines of his faith on a firm soil in the teeth of the   bitterest opposition. Although he was 'a menace to the heretics' as Madhava has described him, his was a charming personality which attracted and pleased those who were near him. A householder, he resigned himself and his all to God, and remained detached from the pleasures and pains of the world. His weal and his woe depended on that of his followers. The culture of *bhakti* among his disciples in the proper manner was his delight. Always busy with his writing of books and the holding of discourses on religion and philosophy, he was not devoid of humour, which often broke forth in the course of his narratives, dramatic works and in common talk.

Sankara brought the message of the religion of love to the   people, released the soul of the common man from the oppressive burden of sacerdotalism and indicated to the individual that his voice could be heard by God if only it rose from a pure and sincere heart. His religious activities formed the basis for the growth of a culture and a literature, both rich and varied. The common man in the backwoods of the valley or on the hills could now embrace a simplified and democratized Hinduism without his having to be looked down upon by the 'high' castes. The new faith had to struggle against Tântricism in its varied and sometimes horrid forms, and it gained sufficient ground within the very life-time of Sankara."

"The great Sankaradeva movement thus brought about a new and comprehensive outlook on life and a distinctly healthy tone to social behaviour. It accelerated the pace of a renascence of literature and fine arts like music and painting. The dignity of the individual endeavour of man as a distinct religious being and not as 'the thrall of theological despotism' was declared. Assam discovered herself as an integral part of the holy land of *Bhâratavarsha*, and gloried in that discovery. The holy books in Sanskrit, the *litterae humaniores* of India, could no longer be sealed to the common man's view by a rigid oligarchy. The use of the local language in expositions of theology and philosophy was in itself a challenge to the erstwhile guardians of secret doctrines, who understood the significance of the challenge and 'protested very much'. The new humanism eyed askance at the numerous blood sacrifices, including the immolation of man, and the nice sacerdotalism thast was the order of the day in Hindu society. The use of Assamese, an *Indo-Aryan* tongue, which formed but an island in a Tibeto-Burman ocean as the medium for the propagation of the new-*Vaishnava* faith led to its emergence as the language of all the people. The ancient Kingdom of Kâmarupa was now undergoing a huge change, and it was having almost a regeneration, political and social, which timed well with the cultural resurgence initiated by Sankaradeva; and the first possibilities of a unified and modern Assam was now in evidence" (1955:378).

References:

Neog Dimbeswar. 1963 *Jagat-Guru Sankardew*. Nagaon, Assam, India: Sreemanta Sankar Mission.

Neog Maheswar. 1967 *Sankardeva*. New Delhi: National Book Trust.

_____1955 *The Early* History *of Vaishnava Faith and Movement in Assam: Sankaradeva and His Times,* Guwahati, Gauhati University.

Chatterjii S.K.1970 *The Place of Assam in the History And Civilization of India,* (2nd Print), Guwahati, Gauhati University.

Late Dr. Maheswar Neog was formerly Professor of Gauhati University and Sankardeva Professor, Punjabi University, Patiala & an Exponent of Sankaradeva Studies.

THE BHUBAN HILL IN CACHAR, ASSAM: ITS ORIGIN AND AFFINITY

Sujit Choudhury

The earliest archaeological site of the Barak Valley of Southern Assam is the Bhuban Hill situated around 23 Kms South East of Silchar. At present the hill is considered as the most important cult-spot of the valley where thousands of pilgrims flocked together to attend the annual fair that takes place on the most auspicious occasion of *Shivaratri*. Obviously it is a *Saivite* cult-spot and the hill earns its present name from this association.

I

A pond is located atop the Bhuban Hill at an altitude of 930 m AMSL. It is a dug out pond at the source of a natural stream that flows down the hill. The pond is held sacred and the visiting devotee pilgrims take holy bath in it before offering prayer to the presiding deity, the *Bhubaneswar* accompanied by his consort *Bhubaneswari*. It is customary to every pilgrim to spend a night at the site and to take at least one nocturnal meal over there.

Just below the peak there is vast flat space in the form of a yard, which is partly canopied by two projected large rocks. A couple of large icons stand beneath this natural roof. These icons are now identified as that of Lord *Bhubaneswar Shiva* and Lady *Bhubaneswari Parvati*. A modest shrine has been constructed close to this that houses a number of broken statues lying scattered in the hills. Fifty years back there were more and more uncared statues in the hills, it is learnt. Natural odds and human vandalism took away many of them. Two of them have been recovered and are currently housed in the premises of the Normal School, Silchar.

Adjacent to the flat plain, there is a small cave that bears the testimony of using it for dwelling purpose in the past. The gate of the cave is well decorated with a stone arch supported by two stone pillars. The arch once had a *Ganesha* image, which either fell apart or was separated, and is now placed little away from it. The craftsmanship related to the arch and the pillars bears an evidence of a well-developed masonry. The roof of the cave is also having curved stone roofs supported by some kind of adhesive.

About 1¼ Km away from this site, there is a big cave that has a long tunnel. The District Census handbook (1961: 8-9) writes a detailed account about this cave in the following: "About 10 ft long and 18"x9" in dimension dug under the rocky hill. This is known as the *Yonidvara* or vaginal passage. One person can crawl through this passage on his breast with difficultly. After crossing this 10 ft long and narrow passage, there is a rectangular yard about 80 ft long and 30 ft high and a wide tunnel absolutely dark. This is known as the *mel-mandapa* i.e., assembly hall. From this hall runs a downgrade path easily passable, for distance of about 400 ft and it leads to the second assembly hall almost of the same size as that of the first. From the second hall another downgrade path from a distance of about 400 ft leads to the third assembly hall. There are two stone images carved on the high wall of the hall but these cannot be identified due to darkness and also due to moss having grown on them.

From the third hall, there is a very narrow passage similarly downgrade for a distance of about100 ft. In the centre of the passage, there is a block of stone with teeth-like nodules protruding on all sides. After a distance of 400 ft there is a triangle stone in the centre of the passage leaving a very narrow slit-like passage on two ends. Only a dare devil can attempt to pass through these slits. Generally nobody dares to penetrate further. It is said that after traveling through this dangerous passage for a distance of half a mile, one can reach a wide rectangular plain yard where there is a *linga* of Shiva. It is also believed that there is an underground tunnel leading upto *Kâmâkshyâ* hill near Gauhati......The tunnel passage and the assembly halls are handiworks of ancient architects of great skill and imagination.

It is hard to believe that the entire tunnels were the handiwork of ancient architects. They are more likely the natural geological phenomena that were expanded and improved by human intervention at an early date. In parts of southern and western India there are number of such natural caves with long tunnels. In the Siju limestone area of the Garo Hills, Meghalaya similar caves with long tunnels are present. It is well known that some of them elsewhere in India were converted into magnificent cave temples, and the cave temple (*Chaitya*) of Kondana in the Paschimghat hills bears a remarkable similarity with the cave of Bhuban hill, much particularly the physical features of the cave-entry of the Bhuban hill with only difference of having impressive structures in the latter (Brown, 1956: Pl. XXV). In the Kashmir Valley the great Amarnath temple with its *Sivalinga* on ice also attract a large number of devotees from different parts of India in June/July before the celebration of *Rakhi Purnimâ*.

II

The huge cave tunnels, the smaller cave house and the sculptural remains are the three phenomena that make the Bhuban hill a composite and fairly complex cultural site. It is logical to believe that the site manifests different phases of cultural developments earlier of which is prehistoric. It is difficult to determine with any amount of certainty a precise demarcation between different phases and to identify the peoples associated with them. Although reconstruction of a reasonable chronology is much difficult, a hypothetical framework may be drawn on the basis of the available evidence.

Kosambi (1983:132) says, "Cultspots on the hill-tops are generally of late high-land origin". Agrarian communities normally occupied low land in the plains and hilltops were of no use to them, and in such a situation pastoralists had to shift to the highlands and hilltops with their flock and cattle under pressure. These pastoralists were nomadic and the Bhuban hill might be one of their seasonal campsites. Normally nomadism and pastoral way of life were associated with a patriarchal society and such a community preferred to have a male guardian deity. Shiva of Bhuban hill might have originated in such a belief of worshipping a male deity amongst the pastoralists who had settled at its hilltop. Pastoralism is essentially related to a seasonal cycle of the year when the community concerned moves in search of fodder for their domesticated animals. Bhuban hill was perhaps one of such camping sites. The traditional practice of spending a night by the visiting devotees at this cultspot might signify a symbolic observance of such a pastoral behaviour of the earliest inhabitants of the region.

No material is available to ascertain the identity of such a group of earliest pastoralists. According to Banikanta Kakati

(1945:10-16), These earliest settlers who laid the foundation of *Shaivite* cult spot were of *Kirâta* origin." On the evidence of Kâlika Purâna, Kakati asserted that Naraka, an adventurer prince hailing from Mithila ousted these Shaivite *Kirâtas* from Kâmâkshyâ hill, which was also a *Shaivite cultspot* originally. According to him such an encounter between the *Kirâta* and Naraka took place in the 2nd Century AD. Kalikâ Purâna reveals the ousted *Kirâtas* from Kâmâkshyâ hill went towards the eastern sea. The *Kirâtas* mentioned in ancient literature were the Indo-Mongloids of the earliest variety.

In another significant observation Kakati said, Naraka should not be identified with Narakâsura of epic Mahâbhârata. Naraka was a fortune-hunter prince from Mithila who played an important role in the process of *aryanization* of Eastern India. To quote Kakati,

> "The Kalika Purana tells the story of a certain Naraka (different from the Naraka of the epics) of Mithila, leading a colonizing expedition into the ancient Pragjyotisha Kingdom. Referring to its previous history, the Purana says that the kingdom (Pragjyotisha) was formally preserved by Sombhu for his own domain. The aboriginal inhabitants were Kiratas with shaven heads and addicted to drink and flesh. A Vaishnavite religious guide (described as Vishnu, his putative father) accompanied Naraka in his expedition. Naraka settled twice-born people within his kingdom and he was enjoined by his Vaishnavite guide not to worship any other deity except Kamakshya, a Yoni goddess. He could not transfer his devotion to any other god or goddess except on the penalty of death. Siva is evidently ignored being classed with other gods. It would appear that the

aboriginal Kiratas were under the protection of Siva, because it has been said that they were expelled to the eastern seas with the consent of Sombhu. Divested of symbolism, this may mean that the Kiratas under their saivite leader voluntarily withdrew towards the eastern sea" (1945:14).

It is not necessary to enter into a debate whether Kakati's contention in it entirety is historically valid or not. There is, however no ground to reject the essence of his argument that the legend of Naraka retains in its some remnants of the tension and conflict associated with the early phase of aryanization of the Brahmaputra Valley. The valley, particularly its western part was inhabited by the *Tibeto-Burman* and *Austric* peoples at that phase the former being the worshippers of male-gods and the later the mother goddesses. The legend of Naraka tells us that the advent of *aryanised* form of culture, economy and polity created some amount of socio-political tension in the region.

There is no need to pre-suppose that the major deity of the Tibeto-Burman people was the Shiva of the *Pauranic* variety. The male god might have some affinities with Shiva and hence the scripture writers equated the former with the latter. The kind of attempted assimilation, absorption or appropriation is very much a living process in the same region. R.N. Mushahary (1989:68), a Boro scholar informs that through the same process, Balhau Bârâi, the leading male deity of the Boros is being identified with Lord Shiva and called *Shiva-Bârâi*.

It needs to be mentioned that the cultural history of the country bears testimony to a general tendency of identifying male-god of the *Kirâtas* with the *Pauranic Shiva*. In the north Bengal the tribal deity- *Jalpeswar* became *Shiva* under the same process. That the mechanism had a wide range of operation is apparent from the reference of Mahâbhârata where Arjuna encountered *Shiva* in a *Kirâta* form. In the Bengali traditional poetry (*Mangalkârya*), *Shiva* is always depicted as associated with the Kocha women of *Kirâta* or *Tibeto-Buman* origin. There are historical references that even after being aryanised, Shiva of this origin retained his dual attributes. In the Koch Royal Records reference has been made that the Koch King Narnarayan was pressurized by his Koch soldiers to arrange for a special *Shiva-puja* in accordance with the tribal mode of adulation. King organized the puja with sacrifice of goat, hogs and buffaloes, and young damsels danced before the deity (Mushahary, 1989:68). It becomes a glimpse of the original mode of worship prevalent among the *Kirâtas* for propitiating their male deity identified with *Shiva*.

It is likely that the *Aryan* or the *aryanised* invaders or immigrants might find these practices crude and dispensable and they might think it desirable to suppress those tribal rites. Perhaps they also resorted to some sort of diplomacy to attend the objectives. It should be remembered that though depicted as religious, these conflicts actually manifest political contest for supremacy. The immigrants perhaps made an alliance with the Austric-speakers of the region that might have an antagonistic relation with the *Kirâtas*. Kakati (1945:11) surmises, "At the same time, to secure easy recognition by aboriginal people, they brought to prominence another local cult, the cult of the Mother Goddess worshipped in the Yoni-symbol, as opposed to the cult of Siva worshipped in the phallic symbol". That this diplomacy succeeded is evident from *Kâlikâ Purâna*, which supports that the *Kirâtas* were compelled to leave Kâmâkshyâ hill once for all and who took refuge on the shore of the Eastern Sea. It is well reasonable to presume that these fleeing *Kirâtas* were the earliest inhabitants of the Bhuban hill. The hill stands in the neighbourhood of Manipur and Mizoram, and according to Niranjan Ray (1952:119) there existed a land route lading to the eastern coastline of Burma and Chitagong Hill via Cachar, Manipur and Mizoram. It is therefore likely that a group of these *Kirâtas* took shelter in the Bhuban hill and laid the foundation of a *proto-Shaivite* cult-spot over there. The traditional belief of having an underground link with *Kâmâkshyâ* hill at Guwahati through the tunnel of the Bhuban hill may be regarded as a popular version of a material and cultural relation, which the early shelters of the Bhuban hill had with *Kâmâkshyâ*. If the data of an aryan invasion of Kâmrupa as presented by Kakati is accepted, then the advent of the Kirâtas in the Bhuban hill might take place in the 2nd or 3rd Century AD. It would be pre-posturous to accept that these *Kirâtas* contributed to the sculpture of the Bhuban hill because there are negative evidences to show that the Indo-Mongloids were yet to attain the ability of stone-sculpturing; however the initiation of the Bhuban hill to a cult-spot of male god, which was later identified with *Shiva* was in all likelihood, was an achievement of these people. Also it may be believed that they widened the natural cave-tunnel to live in as their shelter. Ideally suited other rock-shelters were also used accordingly. And it is perhaps these *Kirâtas* inspired the subsequent *Indo-Mongoloid* migrants to visit the Bhuban hill as a halting station or as a semi-permanent lodging place. Therefore there is every reason to believe that these earliest migrants first undertook the task of expanding the cave at the Bhuban hill.

III

Some of the sculptural relics of the Bhuban hill are crude in appearance and their design and craftsmanship are not at par a developed skill although these human or semi-human images represent some deities. However their anthropomorphic features are clear enough to make their identification possible. People responsible for the production of this phase of culture are difficult to ascertain because of non-availability of suitable evidence. Nevertheless some indirect evidences based on oral tradition say that the *Tripuris* or *Tiprâhs* who in course of time settled in the modern state of Tripura were the people associated with this phase of Bhuban hill culture.

The *Tiprâhs*, a branch of the *Tibeto-Burman* stock also had their earlier settlement in the Brahmaputra valley, more specifically the plains of the River Kopili in the Nagaon and Karbi Anglong districts. In the Royal Chronicle (*Rajamâlâ*) of the Tripura Kingdom mentions that the ancestral abode of the Tripura Kings were the banks of the Kopili River. For certain reason the King and his ten brothers left the Kopili valley and ultimately came to *Khalângmâ* via the upper reaches of the Barabakra (Barak) River, which has been described in the following:

> *Kapilâ nadir tireh bâs châri dilâ*
> *Ekadash bhâi miley mantranâ karilâ,*
> *Sainyasenâ sâney râjâ sthânântarey gelâ*
> *Barâbakrâr ujânerey Khalângmâ bahilâ.*

Khalângmâ is the tribal name of the upper reaches of the River Barak. Perhaps the *Bhauma-Naraka* or the *Salastambha* rulers ousted the *Tiprâhs* from their homeland in the Kopili valley in 7th or 8th Century AD. They traveled though the ancient route used by their kinsman, the *Kirâtas* four or five Centuries earlier, and finally reached the Bhuban hill. Upendra Chandra Guha (1971:20-27) on the basis of some local oral tradition that supports the *Rajamâlâ* evidence says, the *Tiprâhs* once had their sway at the upper reaches of the Barak River. Achyut Charan Choudhury (1911:49-151) attempted to reconstruct the migration of the *Tiprâhs* first from the Kopili valley to the upper reaches of

River Barak , then to southern Sylhet and ultimately to the Tripura State. All these evidences affirm a venture to give credence to the contention that the *Tiprâhs* before finally settled in the Tripura State, had a long sojourn in the Barak valley.

At this stage of presentation it becomes inevitable to draw attention of the readers to another ancient *Saivite cult-spot* of Tripura that is rich in large-scale archaeological ruins. Unokoti hill in Tripura bordering the district of Sylhet in Bangladesh is a renowned *cult-spot* evidenced with different varieties of sculptures including huge rock-cut images. This site is normally associated with the *Tiprâhs* and manifests their zeal for taking up major cultural project at an early date. Regarding the skill displayed in the sculptures of Unokoti, K.N. Dikshit (1986:14) observes,

> "...the style of Unakoti betrays a rudimentary and crude conception of sculpture art and illustrates in remarkable way the canons of primitive art."

Obviously some of the images of the Bhuban hill clearly manifest such 'rudimentary and crude conception'. Gautam Sengupta (1986:15) while dealing with the archaeological significance of the Unokoti ruins directly brings the Bhuban hill in his discussion.

> "In this context, the evidence of sculpture remains from Bhuvan Pahar in South-Eastern border of Cachar District assumes importance. Here one comes across the co-existence of standard Brahminical images carved in eastern Indian idiom and images rendered in a different style. And, significantly Bhuvan Pahar is also a Saivite centre."

Also there are some similar specimens of images in Devatâmurâh hill of Tripura.

It is evident from the instances of Unokoti and Devatâmurâh that the *Tiprâhs* had a special trait for developing hilltops as impressive *cult-spot*. Hence when at an earlier stage they had been dwelling in the upper reaches of the Barak River, it was inherent for them to select a spot for such purposes. They found the top of Bhuban hill already adapted by their predecessors and therefore made it their own *cult-spot*, and undertook the task of decorating it with images.

It may be assumed that the ruins at the Bhuban hill manifest unadulterated tribal features least influenced by the *Brahminical* or *Buddhist* iconography were the handiworks of the *Tiprâhs*. Here the question of a chronology regarding the advent of the *Tiprâhs* in the Barak valley stands relevant. Gautam Sengupta (1986:15) thinks the *Tiprâhs* had been in Cachar in the 15th Century AD. There is however reasons to ascribe an earlier date to the migration of the Tiprâhs from the Kopili valley to Cachar. Some political power as said earlier drove them out of the Kopili valley and in case this adversary is identified, the dating of the Tiprâhs' migration becomes easier. Almost every historian accepts that the Kâmarupa Kingdom emerged as a major political power in the Brahmaputra valley at least during the Gupta period and from a 6th Century inscription, it is gathered that the Kâmarupa King Bhutivarmana had his sway over the Kopili valley. The date of the reign of Bhutivarmana is attributed to 518 AD to 542 AD. The successors of Bhutivarman were powerful rulers and it is unlikely that they lost their grip over the region subsequently. The *Salasthambhas*, who replaced the successors of Bhutivarman in Kâmarupa, also retained their hold over the Kopili valley as evident from the inscriptions issued by Balavarman, Ratnapal and others (Sharma, 1978).

It is reasonable to suppose that in the 6th Century AD the powerful *Bhauma-Naraka* (popularly called the *Varmana* dynasty) established its authority over the Kopili valley by defeating the less powerful *Tiprâhs*. Therefore the *Tiprâhs'* migration from the Kopili valley started as early as the 6th Century AD and their settlement in the Barak valley i.e., around the Bhuban hill cannot be later than the 7th Century AD. The Kâmarupa Kingdom came under the influence of the *Gupta* culture during the period of the *Varmana* supremacy, and *Tiprâhs* perhaps acquired a preliminary knowledge of stone sculpture through their interaction with this culture via Kâmarupa. The tribal artisans in all probability experimented with this newly acquired art form at the Bhuban hill. It should be mentioned, some images of the Bhuban hill strikingly resemble woodcarvings in a medium of stone. Both Perry Brown and Benjamin Rowlands mention similar kind of imposition of designs used for wood-cut in stone-sculpture in early specimens of Southeast Asian sculptures. This trait actually marks the early adaptation of stone sculpture by the tribal artisans. What happened in Southeast Asia is equally possible to happen at the Bhuban hill since both experienced interaction between the *Tibeto-Burman* and the *Brahminical* cultures. It is believed that the early phase of the Bhuban hill sculpture was the handiwork of the Tiprâhs who occupied the region during the 7th and the 8th Centuries AD. No doubt the Tiprahs were responsible for the earliest phase of State formation at this juncture, but still it can be presumed that this rudimentary State provided an economic basis to the Bhuban hill complex for its continued existence.

IV

The devotees in general identify the two life-size stone images at the Bhuban hill as those of god *Bhubaneswar* and goddesses *Bhubaneswari*. Both the images manifest an advanced stage of artistic skill and concept. Some of the broken images have equally refined artistic version. The cave temple near the images also reflects a superior architectural skill and expertise.

The two stone images although identified as that to Lord *Bhubaneswar* and Lady *Bhubaneswari* are atypical to the traditional concept (*Dhyana*) of Shiva and Durga. However Buddhist features in them might make one to identify the male as that of *Lokanâth* and the female a *Tântric* goddess. Some scholars go to identify the female image as a Kuki woman, but this naming is far fetched. Significantly the female has postures and other physical features of a deity with a typically Mongoloid face. Other images too bear some kind of Mongoloid features but they are not as vivid as that of the goddess. It appears that The *Pâla* form of art prevalent in Eastern India effectively influenced the *Tiprâhs* or some allied *Tibeto-Burman* inhabitants at this stage. This stage of the Bhuban hill culture may be attributed to the 10th or the 11th Century AD.

A developed economic support base definitively patronized this developed phase of culture at the Bhuban hill complex. It is not certain yet whether any royal houses in Eastern Bengal rendered any support to this complex. However there is a strong possibility of other kind of patronage in this regard. Nihar Ranjan Ray (1951:119) speaks of an ancient trade route that traversed though Tripura, Jamuna-Baraka valley, Mizo Hills, Manipur to reach Pagan of Burma. The Paltikera Kingdom, which had its centre at Comilla district in Tripura had an intimate trade and political relation with Pagen Kingdom of Burma in the 11th and 12th Century AD, and this trade route was instrumental in development of a close contact between Burma and Eastern Bengal.

The position of the Bhuban hill on this route is much strategic, which clearly demarcates the end of the Gangetic plain in the east and the beginning of the hilly region that continues upto the hills of Burma via Mizoram or Manipur or both. Kosambi (1983:132) shows that ancient cult-spots, temples and monasteries were normally situated in the vicinity of the ancient trade routes. And these sites were selected keeping in view their traditional significance and sanctity. The World's largest Buddha statues were also built through the patronage of the trading communities on its trade route from India and Arab countries in Bamiyan, Afghanistan, which were later destroyed by the Taliban regime in that country. Similarly the famous Madan Kamdev temple complex near Baihata Chariali in Kâmrup was also developed at the patronage of some traders who used to pass by the site where mercantile sojourn took place (Dilip Medhi, 2005: Personal communication). Bhuban hill was quite fit in the pattern and it was natural that this tribal cult-spot was adapted, developed and utilized by the traders who used this track to maintain a link between Bengal and Burma (now Myanmar). In all likelihood the Bhuban hill, like some of the cave temples in Western India was converted into monastery of modest size, which was used as a halting spot of the traders. From the 10th Century onwards the Surma-Barak valley has been under the rule of Buddhist dynasty as evident from the Paschimbhag copper plate of Srichandra of Eastern Bengal. The subsequent

Paltikera dynasty was also the Buddhist. No doubt during this period, the Bhuban hill became a Buddhist cult-spot and the Buddhist affinities of the images now known as *Bhubaneswar* and *Bhubaneswari* are the product of this period. As happened in other places, the Hindus subsequently treated this Buddhist cult-spot as a *Saivite* one. It needs to be mentioned that during the Late *Pâla* period this distinction between the Hinduism and the *Tântric* Buddhism became marginal and thus the conversion of Buddhist deities into Hindu *Shiva* and his lady was simply a question of time.

In conclusion it can be said that the three different stages of Bhuban complex in spite of their differences in execution and style were associated with three segments of *Tibeto-Burman* people who inhabited the region in succession. Therefore the Bhuban complex may be treated as a typical example of the gradual development of *Tibeto-Burman* culture in the Eastern India.

References

Brown Perry. 1956 *Indian Architecture*. Plate No. XXV. Calcutta.

Choudhury Achyut Charan. 1911 *Srihattar Itibritta, Vol. I, Part II*: Pp. 49 and 151. Sylhet.

District Census Handbook, Cachar. 1961. Pp. 8-9.

Guha Upendra Chandra. 1971 Kacharer *Itibritta* (In Bengali - Reprint). Gauhati.

Kakati Banikanta. 1945 Mother-*goddess Kamakshya*. Gauhati.

Kosambi Damodar Dharmananda. 1983 *Myth And Reality*. Bombay.

Mushahary R.N. 1989 Aryanization and Hinduization of the Bodos. *Proceedings of the North-East India History Association.* Shillong.

Ray, Nihar Ranjan. 1952 (1359 B.S.) *Bengalir Itihas* (In Bengali). Calcutta.

Sengupta Gautam. 1986 *Proceedings of the 7th Session of North-East India History Association.* Pp. 14-15.

Sharma Mukunda Madhab. 1978 Inscription of Ancient Assam. Guwahati.

_____

Dr. Sujit Choidhury is a historian, was a former Faculty Member of the Department of History at Rabindra Sadan Girls' College, Karimganj, Assam and was a fellow to the Institute of Advanced Study, Simla.

TEMPLES AND TEMPLE
ARCHITECTURE IN ASSAM

Pradip C. Sharma

There is no dependable evidence of earliest architecture of a temple or an alter of Assam. The genesis of temple building in Indian history has been reframed from the Rigvedic literatures by scholars like Fargusson, Cunninghum, Brown, Vat and Agrawalla who have traced it from the natural caves to the impermanent shades and thence to the excavation of caves and even structural temples in imitation of the earliest timber architecture (Bhattacharjya, 1963:1). Moreover early scripture and travel accounts give evidence of carvings in structural remains of certain old buildings at Sanchi, Bharhut and Mathura (Brown, 1956:Pl. XII). But Assam does not retain any scriptural evidence of its own nor any architectural remains similar to mainland India, which enable us to reconstruct an early phase of architecture in the region. Nevertheless, it must also be admitted that there is no attempt so far been made at important temple ruins at Bamuni Pahar near Tezpur, Deo Parbat near Jorhat and other available ruins lying hitherto in parts of former Assam. Richard a. Engelhardt, UNESCO Regional Advisor for Culture in Asia and the Pacific at UNESCO Regional Office at Bangkok after his visit to Deo Parbat and Bamuni Pahar in December 2000 observed that in all probability the Bamuni Pahar temple could be reconstructed well. Mauro Cucarzi and Patrizia Zolese from Lerici Foundation passed a similar remark after looking at the ruins of Bamuni Pahar in 2002. No doubt there would be huge involvement of finance and time together with the supervision of appropriately skilled expertise and funding from UNESCO, allied agencies and other institutions in India and abroad (Dilip Medhi : Personal communication, 2006). This kind of meaningful exercise preceded by a research would certainly provide knowledge of ancient architecture in this part of India, Dilip Medhi observed.

The Brahmaputra valley of Assam or the former Assam does not find a mention in the *Vedas*. Even the earliest Buddhist scriptures and the *Brahmanas* do not mention about it. Nevertheless the two great Indian epics - the *Râmayana* and *Mâhabhârata* and the *Purânas* recorded *Prâgjyotisa* alias *Kâmarupa* adequately as a monarchical power.

The earliest Indian scriptures mentioned this region as the abode of the *Kirâtas* or *Mlecchas*, indicating that the area was devoid of any temple of the normal Hindu form (Kakati, 1955:1-10). Those communities might have practised some sort of esoteric religion any permanent structure or abode. The religious shrines they established might have been restricted to such simple forms as an altar made of earth or an impermanent shade of bamboo, cane and wood beneath some trees in the form of *Deosâls* (*deo* means gods and *sal* means sanctuary), which still survive in many parts of Assam region. The megalithic tradition, which has been practised even now by some tribes of Assam, might also have been in use since the remotest time. Thus, these religious trends did not evolve in any permanent forms. So, in studying the history of temple architecture in Assam, the *Vedic* form of religion is the only answer.

The time of propagation of *Vedic* tenets in the Brahmaputra valley is not clearly known. However the epics have mentioned the Kingdom of *Prâgjyotisha-Kâmarupa* with *Naraka* as its earliest

King, and Naraka's cedibility for the establishment of forts and temples (Kakati 1955: 9,56,57), the archaeological evidences discovered so far do not indicate anything earlier than 5th century AD. Therefore, the Brahmaputra valley came under the influence of the *post-Vedic* faiths since the time of imperial *Gupta*s in Northeast.

The earliest evidence of the *pro-Vedic* activities in the Brahmaputra valley discovered so far include two stone inscriptions found at the Nilachala hill and Dhansiri valley respectively and they are assigned palaeographically to the 5th century AD. The fragmentary Dhansiri stone tablet inscription, though not complete, mentions the donation of land as an act of piety to one Brahmadutta which adequately proves the spread of the Vedic culture to the fringes of the Naga hills in the 5th century AD. The Umâchala Rock Inscription tells about the establishment of a temple, the first and the only of its kind founded in the entire Brahmaputra valley. The building of this temple may be said to be the dawn of an era of constructional activities in Assam culminating in the appearance of ever increasing number of temples, which in course of time studded the entire Brahmaputra valley in the past.

The Dawn of Temple Architecture in Assam

The famous Kâmâkshyâ *Saktipitha* situated in the Nilachala hill, has the credit to become the first temple in the history of Assam. The earliest legend of the land is associated with *Naraka*, an Aryan prince from Videha in central India, is said to have come to *Pragjyotisha-Kâmarupa* alias ancient Assam and carved out a Kingdom by subjugating the *Kirâta*s (Kâlikâ Purâna:318). In fact *Naraka* appears to be the first Aryan King of the Brahmaputra valley and the *Prâgjyotisha-Kâmarupa* becomes the first Aryan kingdom where he had settled the *dvijas* or the

Brahmins for the first time (Kâlikâ Purâna: 38/124). From the archaeological point of view also, the Nilachala hill has the earliest rock-cut inscription of the region. Further, some of the surviving sculptures and carvings show that the premises of the present Kâmâkshyâ temple on the Nilachala hill bears testimony of one of the earliest stone built temples in Assam.

The Umâchala Rock-Inscription has recorded another cave temple located in the northeastern slope of the Nilachala hill. But the site does not contain a cave nor any temple ruins at present and has two parallel rocks with vertical surfaces facing each other instead and the front of one has this inscription. Written in the *Brahmi* and in Sanskrit language, the content of this inscription is as follows:

maharajadhiraja sri surendravarmana krtam bhagavatah valabhadra svaminaya idam guham.

Here, Surendra Varmana is said to have established a cave-temple for the god *Valabhadrasvami*. This King has been identified with King Mahendra Varman, sixth in lineage, of the Varman dynasty of Kâmarupa. The temple has been mentioned as a cave without any detail desription. It was a natural cave and was restored with a cubical shape to an inside chamber, incising a door-motif in front similar to those done in the 4th and 5th Century Gupta caves of Udaygiri hills at Vidisa. That the Umachala cave-temple followed the Gupta norms can be well surmised by the similarity in the inside space occupied by the floor in between the two standing rocks at the site with that of the earliest caves of Udaygiri. It is also possible that the cave had a structural porch similar to a number of caves at Udaygiri.

The Umâchala Rock Inscription contains the name *Balabhadra*, the deity, which indicates the existence of the *pancaratra* cult in Assam in the 5th Century AD and is supposed to be extinct in the Ganga valley with the emergence of the imperial Guptas. The survival of this cult in this part may indicate that, either the followers of this religion colonised the Brahmaputra valley prior to the advent of the Guptas, or, with the growing popularity of the *Pauranic tenets* with the rise of the Guptas, they might have been driven out from the Gupta empire, whereupon a section had infiltrated into this region. Be that as it may, this unusual fact is not only of great consequence to the history of Assam, it is also of immense importance for the study of Indian history of that period.

Whatever be the size and shape of the Umâchala cave-temple, the fact remains that it is the earliest known *Pauranic* temple of the Brahmaputra valley and as such, is of prime importance for the architectural study of the state of Assam. Further, the contents of the Umâchala inscription tend to show that this edifice did not carry any indigenous or independent element but was modelled after the *pre-Gupta* or early phase of the Gupta architecture. Though we do not have any evidence to show that this piece of architecture served as a matrix to shape the building activities of the subsequent period, it obviously occupies the pride of place as the earliest permanent edifice of the Brahmaputra valley. The *pancaratra* cult was very much in vogue in pre-Gupta period but none of the Gupta epigraphical evidences has mentioned about it nor does any other record prove its survival upto this period. (Majumdar, 1966: 447)

Temples of the First Phase

Though the cave-temple of the Umâchala is the earliest example of temple-building in Assam, it had remained as an isolated instance of temple building in this region, since no other evidence is available about building any other cave temple in Assam during the early medieval period.

The starting point of the history of Assam with conclusive evidence at temple building is the regime of Kumara Bhaskara Varman, who is the thirteenth, and the last King of the first historical *Varman* dynasty of Assam. This King has left behind two copper-Platte charters (Sarma, 1988:10-32 & 38-87), a few fragmentary clay seals incised with epigraph and insignia (Sarma, 1988: 35-37), and some literary evidences as recorded in Banabhatta's Harsacharita and Chinese traveller Hiuen Tsang's travel account. As for the purpose of the two charters, they record the donation of lands to Brahmins only, and they do not refer to any temple. The seals also do not give us any insight into temple building. The Harsacharita relates Kumar Bhaskar Varmas's might as also his participation in the Prayaga religious festivals, but it does not mention anything about temples. It is Tsang's Si Yu Ki which only speaks though succinctly of the existence of temples in Assam. However Hiuen Tsang could locate hundreds of *Deva* temples in the Kingdom of Kamarupa.

In the absence of direct evidences, it is a fact that there are archaeological ruins at a few sites in Assam, the components of which show Gupta features in style and execution. However, none of these ruins are sufficient to conjecture conclusively the entire shapes of the complete structure.

There was probably at least one Gupta temple in the precinct of the Kâmâkshyâ temple on the Nilachala hill within greater Guwahati. Apart from a few sculptures with distinct Gupta features, the area seems to have a good number of building components that had constituted parts of a *post-Gupta* temple (Banerji, 1924-25: 98). Of particular mention is a horizontal scroll of exquisite beauty with exceptional precision, which speaks of an age of supreme maturity. Carved on a fine-grained granite, it contains a sitting figure in the act of issuing from his mouth a torrent of horizontal waves in reverberating profile (Sarma, 1988: Plate XIX). Some other stone pieces with geometric designs might have survived from this temple. At Mikirati, a sparingly populated area about two kilometres north of the Davaka market in Nagaon District, exists remains of several stone and brick temples. The ruins include some mutilated sculptures, which are stylistically placed in the Gupta period. (Prakash, 1977: 54). The sculptures apparently formed parts of a structure and some stone blocks may also constitute the components of a temple.

At Dakshin Barganga, a village near Dokmoka in the Karbi Anglong district, there exists a rock-cut inscription indicating the establishment of an *asrama* (monastery) during the 6th Century AD. The site contains several large rocks lying undisturbed through the ages. Sculptures and brick ruins of much latter time are also seen in that site. Of special significance here are two Saivite *dvarapalas* (door-keepers) who are standing on either side to an entrance comprising two rocks in a parallel position with a width of one metre in between them. About a kilometre east of Dakshin Barganga, and on the top of the Mahamaya hill, exists a rock-cut cave of smaller dimensions with the imitation of an incomplete door-frame incised in front, which is typically Gupta in outline. The site also contains some line-figures inscribed on rock, which are of a later period. Whether it is Mikirati or Barganga or Mahamaya, all of these sites with Gupta evidence constitute parts of the valley of River Jamuna, indicating that the vast alluvium of the close by Jamuna bordered with the Davaka and other ranges of hills of Karbi Anglong was the cradle of a culture, which was typically Gupta in theme and execution. The only lacuna to elaborate the versatility of this phase of production is the numbers of evidences, which are not enough to reconstruct its architectural features elaborately.

The only example of the Gupta idiom, which has survived with most of its features, is the ruins of a brick temple with a stone door-frame discovered at the village Paravatiya in the Sonitpur district (Banerji1924-25: 98-99). As for its structural ruins, only the brick-plinth of the temple has survived, the ground-plan of which consists of a *garbhagriha* (sanctum-sanctorum) circumscribed by a *pradaksinapatha* (circumambulatory path), a *mandapa* and a *mukhamandapa* (porch). Some stone columns along with their base-plates and structural members have also survived inside the *mandapa* indicating that a frame of stone beams and columns supported the roof of this brick structure. That the walls of this brick temple contained some sculptural decorations is indicated by the discovery of a few fragmentary terracotta sculptures at the site (Banerji, 1924-25: 99). The site was exposed by R. D Banerji and a report thereof was published by him in the Annual Report of the Arcaeological Survey of India, 1924-25 (Banerji, 1924-25: 98-99 and Pl. LIV, fig. f). The stone portal found at Dah-Parvatiya is of prime importance as a piece of plastic art of the Gupta period. The door frame exhibits features which are typically Gupta in them, spirit and execution. In its outer profile, the lintel of the frame overshoots the outer vertical lines of the door-jam, which is typical only to that age.

The lowest part of each jam of the doorframe has a pair of female figures in each, identified as *Ganga* and *Yamuna*, the two river goddesses. The *lalatavimba* (central zone of the lintel) contains the figures of Sivalikâsu at the centre and that of *Garudâ*, the vehicle of Visnu. The doorframe is thoroughly carved on its front face with vegetal and human carvings which are very much similar to the Gupta theme and which reveal superb craftsmanship of the Gupta age. In fact, "this portal has been regarded by art critics as one of the best specimens of its class in the Gupta period". (Agrawala,1968: 45) and Gupta art that resulted as an unknown political collaboration between the two co-existing Kingdoms of Kâmarupa and the Guptas that occurred in the 5th-6th Century AD

The building activities of the first phase of Assam thus exhibit the same traits of contemporary developments beyond Gupta dominated mainland India and was destined to dominate the subsequent Centuries.

Temples of Medieval Assam

Development of the Indian temple architecture during the post-Gupta period underwent transition to give birth to the regional styles, and in North India, the temple style gradually evolved to a final form by about 7th Century AD (Brown, 1956: 122 ff and 75 ff.) This is more popularly known as the *nagara* type that embraced the entire northern region of the Indian Sub-continent form Gujarat to the plains of Brahmaputra valley. However, the temples of this period could develop regional elements with *nagara* concept to form separate groups to be known as *Kalinga, Lata* and *Vairata*. Most of the forms excepting the one that developed in Kâmarupa survived to facilitate the study of their individual character, but none of the contemporary *Kâmarupi* creations stood the test of time.

Though toppled and scattered, the remains of the *Kâmarupi* temples retained structural components in plenty that enabled the researcher to know a lot about them. Nevertheless, most of these materials are either half hidden in soil debris or are dilapidated considerably, require careful examination.

The early medieval ruins of Assam are found centring round certain key localities of Assam region, which were usually cities and capitals of its bygone regimes. They are mostly concentrated in areas like Singri (Sonitpur district), Tezpur (Sonitpur district),

Jogijan (Nagaon District) and Dubarani (Golaghat district) without any evidence of inscriptions, inscribed antiquities and dates. However, they retain enough-sculptural and architectural member, which can be stylistically assigned to this period.

Suryapahar, Pancharatna, Paglatek

Suryapahar in the present Goalpara district appears to be one of the earliest places of Assam to harbour the propagation of Hindu culture in eastern India. It is a undulating triangular tract bounded by the River Brahmaputra and its tributary Dudhnai and Krishnai on its north and east, and the low range of hills on its south-west in diagonal position comprising the hills of Suryapahar and Mahadevpahar along with flat alluvial plains retain huge archaeological evidences belongin to early Centuries of Christain era (Prakash, 1977: 50). Early settlers of the Brahmaputra valley established a workshop to model and produce objects of pre-Gupta and Gupta idioms and helped the earlier artists to form a guild of sculptors and carvers who, in course of time shaped a thematically Pauranic art-style, which became indigenous outwardly to suit the taste and temperament of the people. It is also possible that it was Suryapahar, which inspired the growth of many more sub-centres of art and craft in its neighbourhood places of Marnai, Dekdhowa, Pancharatna, Jogighopa, Abhayapuri and Paglatek .

Among the antiquities, the most conspicuous in this region are the votive *stupas* cut out of rocks, the biggest of which measures 2.20 metres in height. In outer profile some of them resemble their proto types of 1st-2nd Century AD and it is not unlikely that they record the propagation of the Buddhist religion of the *pre-Gupta* period to this part of the Brahmaputra valley. Reminiscences of this phase at Pancharatna, and situated on the south bank of the Brahmaputra, 20 Kms down stream of

Suryapahar where votive *stupas* and rock-cut evidences of *dipastamabha* are seen. Another antiquity of importance is a rock-cut image of a *Bodhisvatva* found at Suryapahar, which was initially taken as a Hindu Devi but subsequently identified as the image of *Avalokitesvara* of the Buddhist pantheon.

The phase of Hindu dominance in Suryapahar seems to be of latter origin and does not go beyond the 8th century AD. Apart from rock-cut *Sivalingas*, the site contains a frieze of rock-cut images of Siva and Vishnu in alternate succession, which can be stylistically assigened to 8th Century AD. Depicted in *samapada-sthanaka* posture, the nude Siva images are out in ithyphallic order while the Vishnu images carry prominent *cakras* that are depicted with some amount of distortion to give three-dimensional effect. The portable stone slab from which the name 'Suryapahar' evolved, contains a central figure encircled by twelve other figures in a circle. The central figure is identified as that of the great sage *Kashyapa* and the twelve images as *dvadasaditya*s or the twelve gods representing the twelve months of the year. The slab, being isolated, does not show its connection either with the rock-cut frieze mentional above, or to any structural monument in or near about the spot, but it is likely that it was the ceiling slab of a Surya temple of 9th-10th Century AD. Dilip Medhi informs the writer about a new interpretation of the circularly deities-engraved slab, "The Indo-Swiss joint expendition under my leadership in association with Dr. Eberhardt Fischer in the month of November 1998 rejected the idea of assigning it to sage Kashyapa and the encircling *dvadasaditya*s. Dr. Fischer said the central deity was that of Lord Brahma who was busy in consulting *jyotish* or astronomy with his surrounding *dvadas manasputra*s" (Personal communication, 2006).

Suryapahar also perpetuates the memory of the propagation of Jainism to the Brahmaputra valley, which, in fact, is the only proof of this religion to have been practised here during sometime in the history of Assam not precisely known. The southeast extremity in a large natural cave exists two figures of *Jaina* with a short inscription. The figures are identified as that of the Jåina *tirthankara Rvsavanatha* and the images are paleographically assigned to the 7th -8th century AD. Of late, another images of *Adinâtha* alias *Rvsavanatha* in *dhyanasana* was discovered atop the hill near the cave, the dating of which is yet to be done. Apart from the rock-cut images, it contains a series of rock-cut *stupas* and *Sivalianga,* which co-exist. This apart, the area contains a good number of rock-cut cubical caverns, some of which contain monolithic *Sivalingas*. It is possible that a guild of stone-carvers was formed at Suryapahar or in one of its neighbourhood and practised this craft for Centuries together. Dilip Medhi informs, "Recent archaeological discoveries at Surya Pahar made the Archaeological Survey of India to unearth an elaborate temple ruins at its northwest corner. Another temple ruins occur on the eastern bank of the already existing large pond where the famous portable slab that was wrongly assigned to Surya image was initially discovered. Another rock-cut cave of Dasabhuja, currently protected by the Archaeological Survey of India, which situates on the south-western hill-slope and close to the stream flowing over there. Archaeological Survey of India also unearthed a thick brick wall on the right side of this image" (Personal Communication, 2004).

Suryapahar is the only unique place of Assam where Hindu, *Buddha* and *Jaina* faiths are seen together and is the only place of the state where Jainasm shows its existence during the entire historical period. Some ancient water tanks and ramparts are seen on the flat alluvial lands near Marnai to the north of

Suryapahar up to the bank of river Brahmaputra. Mahadevpahar, a famous place with *tântric* relevance and having ruin of a famous shrine called *Sombheswar devalay* with a *ardha sivalinga* on a *padma-yonipith* in the west has several other spots containing stone and brick ruins. All these make the author to beleive that Suryapahar and it neighbourhood happened to be, like Guwahati and Tezpur, an area of continous settlement for the followers of the major Gangetic faiths which rose to prominence during the first 10th Centuries of the Christian era.

Dekdhowa is about 5 Kms downstream of Suryapahar has a number of rock-cut *sivalinga*s, situated on the steep rock bank of the river Brahmaputra and are closed by an ancient *Majhar* of late Medieval period. The area is currently populated by immigrant Muslims but it requires an intensive survey and further exploration.

At Pancharatna, ruins of a stone temple with some architectural motifs showing post-Gupta influence is located 10 Kms down stream and on the same side of the River Brahmaputra. The evidence of rock-cut *stupas* has already been mentioned. At Jogighopa on the north of River Brahmaputra and facing Pancharatna, exists several rock-cut caverns, some of which contain monolithic pedestals indicating enshrinement of portable images. Hewn out in precipitous rock-faces at levels beyond the easy reach of man from the ground, they appear to be shelters of recluses belonging to Buddhist or Jaina faith.

At Paglatek, ruins of structural buildings can be seen which are indicative of a stone temple of the latter phase of the Gupta period. A horde of gold coins of Gupta era of 7th Century AD having typical Gupta impress were discovered near Paglatek during early seventies of the 20th Century.

Guwahati and its neighbourhood

Guwahati is identified with *Prâgjyotishpur*, the capital of the ancient Kingdom of *Prâgjyotisa-Kâmarupa*. Sculptural ruins since the 7th Century AD are discovered in the present day area. But, being a living city through the ages, it is very difficult to discover anything *in situ* or in an orderly manner to enable one to give a coherent picture of its phases of architectural developments.

Archaeological evidences show that Guwahati witnessed two parallel trends of production in stone, one structural and the other sculptural, mostly hewn out of living rocks. Rock-cut sculptures are mainly seen along the course of River Brahmaputra in places like Dirgheswari, Guwahati water-works, Sukresvar, Aswakranta, Umananda, Urvashi, Karmanasa and Pandunath while a few others are also seen inland. A few of these sites, such as Dirgheswari and Urvashi, retain clear signs of utilising rock faces not only for sculptural art but also for modelling into stairways and sanctum sanctorum. Driving holes in living rocks for inserting columns and dowels are traced in places. Though some of these attempts seem to have coincided in time scale with those of Suryapahar, the emphasis was laid here not on caves or caverns but on superficial depictions. The holes of conspicuous sizes on rocks are indicative of using timber and thatch structures over shrines and places of worship.

Dirgheswari exhibits attempts at modelling a temple complex out of extensive rocky outcrop spreading over almost an acre. The area shows rock-cut sculptures and several cella-floors hewn out on the rock surface. Some of the cella floors show depressions and dowel marks around them indicating existence of a structure over them. A labyrinth of stairways can also be seen in spite of their defacement. Even the brick temple of the late-medieval period, which is in existence at present at this spot was erected on an extension of the same rocky area, originally occupied by a rock-cut cellar hewn out with a few images on its northern wall. In fact, such attempts on rock surfaces by way of levelling surface, clearing passages etc. can also be seen at spots like Guwahati water-works, Sukresvar and at Pandunath. Such attempts are also seen in a good number of spots around the Kâmâkshyâ temple at Nilachal as also at Asvakranta and Umananda. Of particular mention here is a cubical cave hewn out of rock seen in the island of Umananda.

The rocky islet of Urvashi in the midst of River Brahmaputra with a conspicuously modern brick-tower on it, contains an elaborate sequence of sculptures and carvings that reveal an age of busy rock-cut activities. It also contains stairways and platforms, all cut in living rocks. Some foundation lines of structures along with dowel holes can also be seen on the surface of the rock. The most conspicuous among these architectural evidences here is a layout of a structure, which contains an apsidal end similar to the Buddhist *Chaityas* found elsewhere. This type of structure was also popular in Late-Medieval Assam, and its impermanent form can still be seen in the *Neo-Vaishnavite Sattras* of Assam. This evidently is the earliest example of any edifice of this type to be found in Assam, which can be assigned to 9th-10th Century AD, if not earlier.

Of the structural ruins, a few components from the earliest city of Guwahati mentioned already have been preserved in the Assam State Museum. They consist of building blocks incised with different images, such as that of Durga, Nataraja, Vishnu and Ganesh belonging to the 7th-10th Century AD. Most of them are large in dimension and heavy in proportion indicating an earlier age. Some carvings found in the precinct of the Kâmâkshyâ temple on the Nilachal hill also belong to this period. The temple ruins at **Hajo** also contain certain features of this period.

Temple Building in and around Tezpur

Though the plastic art of Tezpur cannot be said to be coeval with that of Suryapahar or Guwahati, there are evidences that can be approximately assigned to the time of the above two areas. Epigraphically it goes back up to the first half of the 9th Century AD but architecturally to 5th-6th Century AD.

Besides the Da-Parvatiya temple mentioned earlier, Tezpur has the credit of containing the earliest structural-ruins of the State. The areas has more ruins, both of stone and brick assigned to the post-Gupta phase. Ruins of a stone temple at Baralimara *Sattra* near Da-Parvatiya are assigned to 8th Century AD. Such ruins were also seen at Garar *Dol* and in areas to the northwest of Da-Parvatiya temple that constitute antiquities of the same phase.

The Maha-Bhairava temple ruins in the heart of the Tezpur town has architectural components, which are typically similar to the pillars found at the Baralimara Sattra. Similar pillars were also found at Bam-Parvatiya, which are now preserved at the Cole Park of the town. All of these antiquities tend to show that Tezpur witnessed a phase of prolific architectural activity since 6th Century AD.

Majgaon on the northern outskirt of Tezpur locatess ruins of at least one temple, which can be assigned to 8th Century AD, if not earlier. Though the components of this edifice are now scattered and are mostly lost, the carvings on the ones that have survived show that it was built by about 8th Century AD. The most important features that these components carry are the sculptures of Ganga-Yamuna, which are incised in the door-jams, but which, from the point of depiction and craftsmanship appears later than those of the Da-Parvatiya temple.

A number of structural components belonging to a period ranging from 8th to 10th Century AD are preserved at Cole Park. Three groups of components belonging to three different edifices are noticed in this collection. Banerji (1924-25) was of opinion that the large structural pieces in this assortment belong to a huge *Sun temple*, the height of which would be about 30 metres. Though Banerji's contention is convincingly based on the figures depicted on the lintels and architraves, his classification of the components as well as the chronological framework cannot be accepted. Though the quality of stone of the largest single lintel and the door jam differs at *Cole Park*, they cannot be of two different doorframes belonging to two different periods as the scholar point out. But from the point of sculptural discipline, structural similarity and dimensional parity, they are indicative of their common origin.

Most of the stone pieces now preserved at the Cole Park were collected from its neighbourhood including the present sites of the Chummery Compound and the District court. It is, therefore, evident that the entire area was having a group of temples of huge proportions that speak of a phase of megalomania of the Kâmarupi Kings who ruled from Harupesvara. Incidentally, two stone columns now flanking the entrance to this Park with their exquisite carvings with proportionate precision speak of an age of the highest plastic perfection.

Bamunipahar temple ruins to the east of Tezpur was probably the last of the phase of this megalomania. Though in complete ruins, the site preserves evidences to show that the hillock on which this temple-complex was designed was shaped into an edifice by way of cutting three terraces and covering its outer slopes with stone masonry. The top terrace of this hillock contained a group of five temples to be known in indological term as a *Pancayatana* temple. The main shrine at the middle of this terrace was a Vishnu temple which was established over a monolithic floor by hewing out a huge rock originally standing at this spot. The ruins of this temple still retain the complete fragments of the door frame which contain *dasavatara* images of Vishnu. The four other temples of much smaller dimensions at the four corners of this terrace are also in ruins save for their monolithic floors and components of their door-frames. The site also retains a large image of Narasimha of the *Pauranic* myth in the act of killing the demon *Hiranyakasipu* on his lap. The second terrace, which exists on the east of the top terrace, is elliptical in its eastern end and contains the ruins of a big edifice centrally, which appears to be identified as the *Vahana-mandapa* (an open structure to house *Garudâ* or the vehicle of Vishnu) or a *naimittikotsavamandapa* (an open structure to be used for enshrining a portable deity in any religious festival associated with the Vaishnavite faith). Another smaller structure little east, and bordering the semicircular terrace, can be conjectured as the *dvaragriha* or the gate-house to this complex. The third terrace of this hillock was laid at the lowest level round the other two and probably served as an ambulatory path for the entire complex. It is also possible, as the density of the stone blocks show as well as the side-slopes of the different terraces warrant, that all of them including their peripheries were laid with a layer of stone blocks that turned the hillock into a massive stone-masonry monument. The style of sculptures and carvings of this ruin reveals it to be slightly later in all probability than the Surya temple near Cole Park, and may be assigned to the close of 10th

Century AD. This temple complex is presumed to be the last of a phase of a construction undertaken by a sub-family of the Kâmarupi Kings who had their rule from Hadapeswara alias modern Tezpur from the beginning of 9th to mid 10th Century AD.

Greater Singri

The Singri is a small hill range on the north bank of River Brahmaputra. It is about 12 Kms south of the Dhekiajuli township in the Sonitpur district. It is linked with the National Highway 51 via a gravel road that passes through tea gardens.

Stone and brick ruins are located in an extensive area north of the Singri hills. From Bhora Singri in the east to the Murabhoga Gaon in the west is a flat area of about 8 sq. Kms that retains scattered ruins of yore and, which can be assigned to a period ranging from about 9th to 12th Century AD.

Bhora Singari is rich with ruins of several temples. Some sculptures and carved stones out of these are gathered at a place and they speak of an age of perfectly talented craftsmanship. The sizes of door components including architraves show that these temples were of medium height, but definitely not less than 10 metres.

The largest edifices comprise the ruins of two temples, just towards the north tableland of the Singri hill. Popularly known as the *Viswakarma Mandir*, these ruins retain the plinths and other, which are really colossal in proportion in the perspective of Assam temple architecture. Two magnificent ceiling slabs, one of them is embossed with a *Visvapadma* motif are worth cited. The cella floors of the two temples are monolithic and might have been hewn out of *in situ* rocks. Other components including the *Khapuri*, carved architraves are also large in proportion. Thus, the massive ceiling slabs including the existence of parts of the *mastaka* (pinnacle) show that the temples were top-heavy in design, which, in all probability, was the cause of their collapse during the time of some earthquake and most probably that of 1950.

Guptesvar temple represents another structure in greater Singri ruins and belongs to a later period. However, we have reasons to believe that the plastic activities of Singri were continuous during the entire Early Medieval period that ended with the close of the 12th Century AD.

The Kapili Valley

The valley of the turbulent River Kapili, a tributary of the River Brahmaputra reveals another chapter of temple architecture of the Assam region. Kopili originated in the lofty North Cachar hills, flows in a north-westerly direction and join together with rivers as the like Diyung, Jamuna, Barapani, Kalang and merges with the Brahmaputra.

Juginadi in the form of Ox-bow Lake is an abandoned course of Kapili. The middle portion of this course measuring about 3 Kms stretch flank four archaeological sites known as Rajbari, Nanath, Sankhadevi and Sibpur. All of these sites are badly ravaged by floods and human beings to a great extent in the past. However, the plinth portions of them have survived these days, and some of them have already been exposed and preserved by the Directorate of Archaeology, Assam.

At Rajbari, a group of six stone temples enclosed by a massive brick rampart is seen. Though erected in two parallel sets of three, they do not belong to a single period of time and that is reflected in their dissimilar layout. In fact, the shape of the ground plan, the stylistic features of sculptures and carvings, as also craftsmanship show that their period ranges from 9th century to 12th Century AD. A small Buddha image inscribed with the name of *Devapala* was found in the same locality, which is palaeographically assigned to 8th Century AD. A large image of Tripura Bhairavi in fragments was also discovered belonging to 11th Century AD.

Three more ruins in unilinear alignment are also seen beyond its eastern rampart. These brick ruins are now located within private residential compounds. From the extent of the ruins, as also the size of bricks, the group seems to be of a later date and not earlier than 13th Century AD.

Nanath contains ruins of eight temples. All of these temples are built in brick masonry save for their doorframes and columns used in the *mandapas*. The temples stand in two alignments in north-south direction. The western group contains five temples while the eastern group has three. Features of these temples are stated below:

- Temples are not of equal sizes.

- Each of them consists of a *garvagriha* and a *mandapa*. Two of them appear to have *mukhamandapa* as indicated by the existence of mutilated walls in front.

- They are small in the south and show a general tendency of enlargement towards north.

- The temples in the north contained an additional plinth known as *pista* or *jagati* in Indological term. This indicates that the temples in the north were affected by flood of River Juginadi which, does represent the ancient course of River Kapili.

- All these temples enshrine *sivalingas* which look all alike in shape save for their pedestals (*Yonipitha* or *Yantra*), which are either round or rectangular.

- The outer walls of two of these temples contain a decorative band of terracotta panels with motifs of gods, goddesses, flora and fauna.

- All of the temples do not seem to represent a singular phase of construction.

- On the basis of the terracotta sculptured designs and other structural features, the earliest of them can be assigned to the mid 7th Century AD.

The Sankhadevi ruins consist of three stone temples. Their sophisticated structural components with sculptural perfection reflect an era of plastic excellence. Of particular mention is the huge doorframe now lying on the northernmost mound that has superior workmanship of ornamention with sculptures and carvings. In fact, a Devi image in the *lalatavimba* of the lintel is the source from which the name of the site was derived. The ruins seem to be of 10th - 11th Century AD.

At Sibpur ruins of two stone temples are seen. Architecturally they resemble the ruins at Rajbari, but the site needs exposition before any precise assessment can be given.

The Kenduguri *Beel* is another dead course of river Kapili. It exists roughly 300 metres south of the Juginadi. Several other ruins are seen on the northern side of this *beel* of which the Dakshin Kenduguri is the most eye-catching. It is southwardly contiguous to Nanath. The temple was erected on an artificial earthen mound with brick, about 6 metres in height, and consists of a *sanctum sanctorum* with a *mandapa* in front. It is similar in plan and execution to that of Nanath.

An extensive area criss-crossed by Rivers Juginadi, Kenduguri, Nabhanga and Warigandeng was a cradle of cultural pursuits that once made it into an area of intense building activities. The supple Kapili attracted people and blessed them with surplus crops in its valley, and its flood also equally destroyed the human settlement and the affluent temple complex. Numerous remnants of brick and stone ruins found in the eroded banks of this region prove such devastation in the past.

Antiquities of the Jamuna Valley

The Jamuna Valley is cusp shaped; the low hill ranges of the Karbi Anglong fortify its curvilinear northern boundary. River Jamuna flows across the hills in a south-westerly direction with its tributaries Harina, Dikharu and Dimaru. Jamuna is a tranquil river compared to Kapili. It has a larger fertile alluvium and is navigable only in the summer. These two qualities attracted agrarian community to live in its valley. Settlers of Jamuna valley built beautiful temples with carvings and sculptures of exquisite beauty, the evidences of which survive up till now in the entire valley including the fringes of hills. The antiquities in Jamuna valley can be traced back to about 6th Century AD.

Mikirati is a remote village near the Dabaka hill range. It is a Kilometre away from the Jamuna and is about 10 Kms from Jamunamukh, the confluence of the Jamuna and the Kapili, which is inhabited by the Karbis. The ruins of the area can be dated to 5th-6th Century AD. S. K Saraswati discovered here a few mutilated sculptures and assigned them to the Gupta period on the basis on sculptural styles. The Barganga Rock Inscription near Dokmoka carries great importance in the reconstruction of the Early Medieval history of Assam. It is a 6th century AD inscription and records about the establishment of an *asrama* (monastery) during the reign of Mahabhuti Varman, 6th in the lineage of the Varman dynasty of Kâmarupa. Written in *Brahmi* script and in *Sanskrit*, the inscription states that,

*svasti sriparamadaivata paramabhattaraka maharaja
dhirajasvan edhajajinaha sribhutivarmasya padanam
ayuskama visayamatya avagunasya idam asramam.*

It says the performance of the holy act of establishing a monastery by the minister of states, named Avaguna, with the intention of the King's long life. The inscription may have several implications. The establishment of an *asrama* by a minister may indicate annexation of this region to the Kâmarupa Kingdom, which up till then might have constituted an independent country known as Dabaka, as mentioned in the 4th Century AD Allahabad inscription of the Gupta Emperor Samudragupta (340-380 AD). As the inscription wishes a long life for the King, it may also indicate the chronic ailment or a state of very old age of the King. Further, the mention of a *Visayamatya* may also indicate the gubernatorial set-up of the time when *Vasayas* (i.e. the states or the districts) were put under separate *amatyas* (ministers). The inscription that occurs in the midst of the Jamuna valley is also indicative of the extent of the erstwhile Dabaka Kingdom that probably covered the entire plains of the Kapili-Jamuna Doab and also parts of lowly hills of Karbi Anglong district.

The valley including the bordering foothills of the Jamuna valley abounds in archaeological remains. Antiquities are available at Akashiganga, Burhiganga, Mahamaya Barganga, Burhagosain Thân, Sarthe Rongphar Gaon, Charlok Pathar, Phulani, Devasthan, Maudanga, Pandit Ghat and many localities along Dikhara and Dighalpani rivers. The ruins cover several Centuries starting with that of Mikirati ruins and Barganga inscription of 4th-5th Century AD. All of these ruins point to the fact that they were Brahmanical in theme and spirit and the temple structures were *nagara* in style. Rather, it appears to be an extension of architectural productions that took shape in the Ganga valley during the Gupta and the *post-Gupta* times.

Developments of the Dhansiri Plains

Archaeological evidences show that the expanse of building activities of the imperial Guptas extended to the valleys in upper reaches of River Dhansiri, a tributary of the Brahmaputra in Upper Assam. Beautifully curved images of the Hindu deities, mostly that of Visnu have been discovered in numbers in the greater Barpathar region that ranges in age from 7th to 9th Century AD. Some of them include rock carvings. The plethora of sculptures includes other gods and goddesses as *Ardhanarisvara*, Siva, some unidentified deties, some of which may be assigned to 11th-12th Century AD. Deopani Devalaya, a temple complex of Dhansiri plains houses several sculptures discovered from its neighbourhood, the largest among which being a four armed Durga image. Other available images kept in the Ahom gaon temple near Sarupathar, a beautifully sculptured Siva image at par excellence needs special mention. In addition to Barpathar-Dubarani region of the same valley shows extensive use of bricks to limited number of sculptured terracotta panels.

The architectural activities of the Dhansiri Valley are yet to be completely explored and exposed to conjecture its type or style. But the present evidences tend to show its inclination towards brick-masonry appearing at several places of Assam region.

Temple building under the *Kamarupi Pala*s:

The twenty-one monarchs of the Salastamba dynasty left a legacy to their successors, the *Pala*s of Kâmarupa, which was utilised by them most scrupulously and in its perfect form. The *Salastambha*s made buildings with grandiose in planning and larger in dimensions. They consisted of bigger stone blocks, the most conspicuous of them being the door components, architraves and the ceiling slabs without any use of bricks and form a group. Another set of temples with brick and stone make a separate group of *Pala* architecture, which studded the entire Brahmaputra valley with a series of temples although none of them survived intact. Probably, temple structure of smaller stature including exuberance of ornamentation of inner and outer profiles also marked this age.

The *Palas* came to power in mid-10th Century AD. They had their capitals at Prâgjyotishpura, Durjaya and Kâmarupanagara in different times, the locations of which differ according to different historians; however a common opinion refers it to an area in and around the modern city of Guwahati. The period, as is seen from the available archaeological evidences comprising inscriptional and architectural mark an increased temple building throughout Assam region in general and intensive in certain core areas in particular. As in the case of the imperial Guptas, when all the minor deities of the Hindu religion received considerable importance due to an intense royal patronage, so the Palas seem to have encouraged all sects of Hindus, resulting in building of numerous temples. Probably *Purânas* and *Tantras* influenced the people that resulted in construction of more temples to enshrine manifold aspects of gods and goddess. However, none of these temples has survived intact in heaps of ruins with different structural features that are hardly enough to conjecture the details of its architectural form.

The ruins of the Pala temples invariably reveal a *nagara* outlook with *ratha* type of ground plan. But structural components show that the *sanctum* was of different shapes like square, rectangular, octagonal and round. As for the shape of the *sikhara*, it appears the *rathas* usually in case of *nagara* temples, but the *sikhara* of the *mandapa* attached to the *vimana* is made in the form of the *pidadeul* as seen with most of the Orissan temples. Normally, the temples consist of only two chambers, i.e., the *garbhagriha* and *mandapa*. But, the existence of a *mukhamandapa* is also seen in a good number of temples. The use of a *jagati* similar to the Khajuraho temples rarely occurs.

Guwahati and its neighbourhood contained a number of temple ruins of 10th-12th Century AD. Almost all the standing temples of today are reconstructed under patronage of the regimes of Koches and the Ahoms over the foundations of the earlier ruins. Even part of the old *garbhagrihas* and their floors are retained intact. Ruins of Pala temples are seen at Tezpur, Biswanath, Jogijan, Maudanga, Devasthan, Akashiganga, Dokmoka, Chaigaon, Madan-Kamdev, Marnai, Abhayapuri, Khairabari, Baman and in many more areas scattered all over Assam region. The temples can be identified from the stylistic feature of the sculptures and carvings as also from the architectural elements of the structural remains.

At least nine Pala temples are located at Madan-Kamdev near Baihata-Chariali in Kâmrupa. They are spread along the ridge of an isolated hill locally known as Madan-Kamdev on the southern edge of an ancient channel. Most of these temples have been completely pilfered and their well chiselled but plain outer components have been shifted elsewhere, retaining only the rough core-masonry with their basements. However, the heavier architectural members like doorsills, door-jams, lintels, image-pedestals and *gajavyala* motifs in a few of them have survived. The shrine, which has its plinth and part of the vertical walls intact is the westernmost structure called the Madan-

Kamdev temple. It is a living temple with a large *Uma-Mahesvara* stone image in *alingana* posture enshrined inside it. The outer walls of this structure retains few horizontal stone blocks that register depiction of human and divine figures in different postures and the lowest one consists entirely of *kirttimukha* motifs, which girdle the temple including the *mandapa* in the form of a decorative band. A peculiar architectural feature in this temple is that three of its sides are provided with a big projecting niche each, containing a large image in each of them. Of these, the image in the northern niche retains only its lowest part consisting of soles of feet, and a jackal and a vulture below it. The fragmented southern sculpture retains all of its features. It is a youthful *devi* image having three human faces and is sitting on a human corpse which is being devoured by a jackal and a vulture. The image in the western niche is similar in all respects to the above one but its three faces- the central one depicts a human while the other two represents a lion and boar. The *devi* figures in this temple emphasizes female parts in prominence even though the presiding deity is that of *Uma-Mahesvara*. This peculiarity in particular, including other decorative features, this temple may be identified with the temple of *Mahagauri-Kamesvara* mentioned in the Guwakuchi copper-plate charter of Indrapala, the Kamarupi Pala King (circa 1060-1085 AD). It may also be mentioned here that the name Madan-Kamdev is a misnomer which has evidently been derived by some villagers from the neighbourhood in the recent past on being influenced by the *alingana* pose of Uma-Mahesvara image, as also by some erotic sculptures on act of coitus or *maithuna*. Madan-Kamdev also contains a phase of construction with bricks, the ruins of which are seen on the eastern part of the Madan-Kamdev hill. An archaeological exploration under the guidance of Dilip Medhi in

1998 located a best piece of temple ruin with elaborately shaped *sivalinga* and *yonipith* (Medhi, Personal communication, 1999). Medhi informs this writer that this place was entirely communicable by the ancient channel behind the Madan Kamadeva temple complex, which could receive mercantile boats from River Brahmaputra, and the temple complex of this place could develop due to the patronage of the trading communities passed during their voyage via this place. Richard a. Engelhardt, UNESCO Regional Advisor for Culture in Asia and the Pacific, visited Madan Kamadeva in December 2000 with Dilip Medhi and observed that it no doubt developed due to the patronage of the trading communities who used the hill as a commercial hub of agriculture and other produces of the adjoining localities (Medhi, Personal communications, 2003). Medhi said a similar view was also received from Dr. Mike Robinson of Sheffield Hallam University, UK. Therefore the entire ruins of this place need careful exposition along with a research into the agricultural proficiency of the people of the region before a fruitful assessment of the entire complex is arrived at.

Probably, the Pala phase had started with stone masonry, which was replaced by bricks towards its closing period. The only undamaged plinth of the region in bricks belonging to this period identified with certainty is the *Siddheswara* temple at Sualkuchi in Kamrup. Though this polygonally domed brick temple is typically Late Medieval, and is assigned to the Ahom King *Svargadeva* Siva Singha (1714-1744 AD), its *pancaratha* plinth appears to have retained its structural style and form of 11th-12th Century AD. Some natural calamities ruined the temple, which was later rebuilt with bricks, and this contention is also supported by the discovery of a few terracotta images belonging to 11th-12th century AD.

The following features of temple architecture of the Palas make a separate class as against their predecessors:

● They grew smaller in stature.

● They became more numerous

● A tendency of exuberant ornamentation appears both in sculptures as well as in their different structural components within the body of the temple, which were absent in earlier forms.

● The quality of stone deteriorated because of an increased demand for more temples and also because of time constraints and the labour involved.

● Brick-masonry increased towards its closing phase. An easy handling of this new building material brought an advantage to expedite building construction to a large extent.

That the Pala period of Kâmarupa ushered in an age of flourishing plastic activities can be known from two conspicuous facts,

(i)   the temple of this period are found in groups in several localities of this Kingdom and

(ii) sculptures of innumerable deities are found in this period, which does require an intensive iconographic research.

Both these facts clearly show that the Brahmanical faith of this period was divided into numerous sects, which indirectly supported compilation of many more scriptures prescribing separate ritualistic patterns for individual deities of Hindu religion.

Architecture of the Twelfth Century

First half of 12th Century AD registered the climax of the classical phase of temple building in Assam region, so the closing of this century seems to have entered into an age of profligacy and degeneration. Departure of the powerful *Palas* in the second quarter of this century brought to an end of royal patronage in the field of temple construction. Moreover, political instability (Choudhury, 1996: 246) must have compelled the guilds of artists and artisans to disband and disperse, resulting in continuous fall both in the quality and quantity of the building activities. Thus, by the turn of the Century, the architectural activities of the medieval period entered into an age of darkness till it emerges again under the late medieval monarchies of the Brahmaputra valley by about 15th Century AD. This new phase of the late-medieval period could not however revive what the Palas and their predecessors achieved.

Inavailability of information and lack of material evidence to complete the history of the building activities of the period succeeding the fall of the *Palas*, there is reasons to believe that temple constructions were restricted to need of eminence only, devoid of annexes and ornamentations. Its initial stage has *rathas* and the *tharas* that followed at par tradition and masonry skill only, but the walls and the *sikharas* grew plain with limited numbers of *devakosthas* on them. With time the structures became square or polygonal in ground plan and gone without *tharas* in most cases. Rather they became more functional.

One of the simplest temples of *post-Pala* period but of earlier idiom, has probably survived in the stone-built Guptesvara temple of Singri in the Sonitpur district. It is a *pancaratha* temple with all the features of a *nagara* shrine. Its decorative elements on outer surface remained minimum and plain. It has a single *devakostha* on its *bhadraratha* that initiated the main temple itself. The only conspicuous element generally found in the other temples of the region, is the use of double *amalakas*, both in the main *mastaka* as well as in the *angasikhara* of the temple.

The ground plan consists of four chambers, such as, the *garbhagriha*, two *mandapas* and a *mukhamandapa*, all in an east-west alignment with the main doors on the west. All the doors are provided with a stone doorframe ornamented with medieval motifs. Of special mention here is the structural arrangement of the ceiling of the first *mandapa* that was constructed over four columns, placed centrally over the floor, with an elaborated system of cruciform pillar-capitals, beams and concave corner slabs incised with *kirttimukhas*. They evidently exhibit the reminiscences of a bygone tradition of classical vintage dwindled by that time. Temples were thoroughly restored during the late-Medieval period through patronage of Ahom Kings when the three lacerated domes of the *mandapas* were covered with a single *do-sala* roofing in brick-masonry, leaving their inside structures intact. Incidentally, this is the only structure of the region from the early Medieval times, which in spite of its laceration and losses, could stand somehow to exhibit Medieval features in original forms in them.

Epilogue:

The evolution of the temple architecture in Assam is as vague as that of the other parts of India. Existence of autochthonous tribes including their religious beliefs and rites and rituals to this date tend to show that from time immemorial impermanent forms of shrines and temples continued throughout the historical period of Assam region. But, unlike the Indian architecture this region does not have instances to show that the earliest permanent architectural buildings were copied from the impermanent traditional forms. Therefore the anthology of temple architecture in Assam region on the basis of available archaeological evidences commences with the beginning of the regime of the imperial Guptas when architecture received active and sustained patronage to construct structurally standard and aesthetically beautiful temples.

In absence of a formerly strong and developed architectural tradition, the Guptas started their temple building with the excavation of caves at Vidisa by the second half of the 4th Century AD. The earliest instance of any temple building in Assam is a cave-temple of circa 4th-5th Century on the eastern slope of the Nilachala hill. The earliest extant structural ruins of a temple of the region are the Da-parvatiya temple which retains Gupta features of 5th- 6th Century AD in theme and execution. The Centuries succeeding this time show temple ruins which from the point of architectural forms and other ornamental features, are similar to the progressive features of Brahmanical temples of India. Even the sculptural depictions and carvings did not deviate from what was followed in case of the other parts of mainland India.

A conspicuous point of difference between the architectural forms of the Salastambha dynasty (7th-10th Century AD) and Pala dynasty (10th-12th Century AD) is that the Salastambhas developed a trend of megalomanic zeal while the *Pala*s increasingly built temples of smaller stature. Another point of difference is that the former temples restricted their ornamentation to the doorframe, architrave and *devakosthas* only, while the latter extended the embellishments to the domes, the cornices, and even the *sikharas* in certain cases. As for the ground plan, both the periods seem to have confined to the three-chamber principle consisting of the *garbhagriha*, the *mandapa* and the *ardhamandapa*. The use of a *jagati* cannot be said to be altogether absent.

The *Pala* architecture in their latter phase shows increasing use of bricks. Even terracotta sculptures found ever-increasing use to decorate the walls of the temples, Bricks were also used for boundary walls in the form of thick ramparts around a temple or a temple complex. In this context it may also be surmised that even though the *Salastambhas* preferred stone for temple building and bricks for ramparts.

With the exit of the Palas by about the second quarter of the 12th century AD, the early medieval temple architecture of

Kâmarupa suddenly lost its momentum. This is because of the prevailing political instability and the consequent disintegration of the large Kingdom and even anarchy in parts of former Assam, which compelled the traditional families of masons and sculptors to give up their profession or leave the country due to the lack of Royal or other patronage and required protection. The only worthy instance of this period is the Guptesvar temple of Singri, which, though contains a fully developed ground plan with four chambers, is simple in implementation.

With the end of the 12th Century AD the Kâmarupi temple architecture entered into an abyss of darkness till it re-emerged under the late-medieval rulers of Assam in an entirely new garb.

References:

Agrawala P.K. 1968 *Gupta Temple Architecture.* Varanasi.

Banerji R.D. 1924-25 *Annual Report of the Archaeological Survey of India.* New Delhi: Archaeological Survey of India.

Bhattacharjya T.P. 1963 *Cannons of Indian Art.* Calcutta.

Brown P. 1956 *Indian Architecture* (Buddhist and Hindu periods). Calcutta.

Choudhury P.C. 1966 History of Civilization of the People of Assam (2nd Edition). Guwahati: Historical and Antiquarian Studies, Assam.

Kakati B.K. 1948 *Mother Goddess Kamakhya.* Guwahati.

_____ 1955 *Purani Kamrupar Dharmar Dhara* (in Assamese) Pathsala.

Majumdar R. C. (Edt.) 1960 *The Age of the Imperial Unity.* Bombay.

Saikia C. P. (Edt.) 1977 *PRAKAS,* (Assam Publication Board's monthly bulletin in Assamese). Guwahati.

Sarma P.C. 1988. *Architecture of Assam.* New Delhi

Sharma M.M. 1978 *Inscriptions of Assam.* Guwahati: Gauhati University.

Kalikapuranam 1984 (1978 AD) Acharyya Panchanan Tarkaratna (Edt). Calcutta.

Dr. Pradip C. Sarma is currently the Director, Research Council, Vivekananda Kendra Institute of Culture, Guwahati 781 001. Earlier he served the Directorate of Archaeology, Assam.

FORESTRY AND WILDLIFE
HERITAGE OF ASSAM

Pramod Goswami

The heritage of a people originates from its history, culture, religious beliefs and civilization. The name of modern Assam in ancient times was Kâmrupa, descriptions of which are available in historical accounts and the Purânas. Ancient Kâmrupa comprised of small domains such as Kâmrupa, Sonitpur, Kundil, Hirambâ, Jayantipur, Manipur and a few other smaller territorial domains of Kings and chiefs. Afterwards these domains collapsed, the entire region began to be known as Kâmrup (Barbarua, 1997).

Ancient Kâmrup was a Hindu inhabited region, as can easily be surmised from the ruins of innumerable Hindu temples, interspersed with many tribal areas, some of which through contact, absorbed into Hindu faiths and beliefs and few became Hindu completely. The Jayantiyâs of Meghalaya were not a primitive tribe as were some of the others. Their dress was till recently fully Indian. They worshipped the Hindu deity Durga at the Durga temple at Jayantipur. So is the case with the Meitiei Manipuris and the Bishnupriyâ Manipuris of Manipur and erstwhile Cachar district of Assam.

Buddhism did not spread to Assam from the ancient Buddhist centres in Central India. The religion came to Assam with the Ahoms (1228 AD) led by Sukâphâ who "came down to Assam with 1080 men, 300 horses, 2 elephants" (Waddel, 1901).

During the Ahom rule of about 600 years, there were many pockets of Buddhist population in Assam. But after the formal acceptance of Hindu religion in 1654 AD by King Jayadhwaj Singh, the Buddhist population in Assam declined. The Tai language is now nearly extinct, being confined only to the priests and "it is strange that no trace of Buddhism is to be found in the religion of the Ahoms" (M'Cosh, 1837). Because of these reasons, no edicts of Buddha, or the Lion Capitol of the Ashokân Pillar has been found in Assam.

HINDU AND BUDDHIST ATTITUDES TOWARDS FORESTS AND WILDLIFE

Hindus throughout the ages have shown respect to trees and animals in the same way that they show reverence to God or demigods (*devatâs*). Killing of any form of life is also prohibited in Buddhism and Jainism. The Hindus worship many trees –e.g. several species of Ficus (*Anhat, Bot* and *Dimaru*) and many trees e.g. Ashoka (*Saraca Indica*) Bakul (*Mimosops Elengi*) Arjuna (*Terminalia Arjuna*) and Baruna (*Crataegus Sp.*), which with their handsome foliages and flowers make the environment serene and joyful. Many medicines are extracted from the leaves, fruits and bark of these trees. The Hindus throughout the ages have assigned religious status to innumerable animals and birds, from the lowly mouse to the mighty lion, the majestic peacock and the *Garuda*. Many of them are assigned as the mounts or *vahana* of God and the demi-gods of the Hindu pantheon.

Prater in his book *The Book of Indian Animals* says that as many as thirty different mammals are mentioned in the *Vedas*, associating them with the demi-gods of the Hindus. Vishnu, the Supreme God, has the mythical bird, *Garudâ*, as his *vâhana* or vehicle. The favourite diet of *Garuda* consists of snakes. Indra, the King of heaven and the god of thunder uses the elephant named *Airawat* as his vehicle. The *Hanuman* monkey (*Langur*), popularly known as *Bajrangavali* is worshipped in nearly all parts of India. The tiger is mentioned in the Vedas. Mighty lion is the vehicle of the goddess Durga; the mongoose, predator of snakes is depicted in the Mahabharata as a wise creature who gave words of wisdom even to Judhisthira, the eldest Pânadava and the wisest King in the epic of Mahabharata. Saraswati, the goddess of art and learning always sits on a white swan; the deer is associated with Brahma, the creator, and Mahadeva, the destroyer, wearing garlands of snakes, rides on a bull (*Nandi*). The Supreme Creator, Vishnu, in one of his incarnations as a boar (*Varâha*) rescued the mother earth from deluge at the time of creation. The *Dasâvatâr*, the doctrine of ten incarnations names *Matsya*, the fish as the first incarnation, and subsequently *Kurma*, the *tortoise*, *Narasingha* (half-man, half-lion), the *Varâha* (boar) and *Bâmana* (dwarf or pygmy). The resemblance of this doctrine, however vague to Darwin's theory of evolution is striking. Vehicle of god *Agni* (Fire) is the goat and that of *Varuna* (god of water) is a *Magara* (crocodile). *Ganesha*, the god of wisdom, prosperity and who takes away obstacles, has an elephant's head.

It is noteworthy that nowhere in any ancient Hindu scriptures, animals are depicted as the enemy of man. The sages and the hermits used to live inside forests peacefully. The animals neither harmed them, nor did they have to kill anyone for their safety or food. When the Kings took to *Vânaprastha* (renunciation), no wild animals attacked them or not even bothered. They lived in total harmony with nature, depending on vegetarian diets and on milk. Kings in ancient India, and the rulers during the Mogul period used to go for hunting (*Mrigayâ*) not for mere enjoyment, but to keep themselves fit and alert for warfare and combats, and to procure hides and skins used as prayer mats and special garments like armour and shield. It is to this day that the blue cow (*Nilgâi*) and the peacock are sacred organism to the Hindus, who do not kill them despite the tendency of these creatures to damage crops. The noble qualities of animals as narrated in various storybooks of ancient and medieval India were held as examples to be followed by mankind, especially in teaching children about the noble qualities that ought to be cultured. The *Panchatantra* and the *Hitopadesha* are the examples of such literature that have inspired Hindus and Buddhists for ages to acquire virtues from animals also. Snake worship is not uncommon amongst the plains tribes of Assam region – the Kâcharis, Rabhas and the Khasis and also the Assamese who live in adjacent areas. Snakes are considered disciples and soldiers of goddess *Manashâ*. Community *puja*s are performed to propitiate the goddess before the onset of the monsoon so that the villagers are protected from snakebites during the summer. *Nâg-panchami* is one of such occasions. There are a few snake temples in south India. A large number of snakes including cobras reside in these temples, staying mostly behind the elevated area where the deity's throne is kept. The priest feeds the snakes with milk in saucers at a fixed time of the day when they come close to the priest. The people from the nearby areas also come to offer *pujâ*s to the snakes to avoid threatened or impending calamities.

THE TRIBAL HERITAGE

The primitive tribal communities of India, understand through observation the intricate relationship between forests, which, in fact forms the modern scientific concept of a hydrological cycle. The Jaintiyâs of Meghalaya conserve sacred groves and the streams flowing through them to maintain the perennial supply of water to paddy fields located at the lower slopes of the hills. These groves at a high altitude comprise mostly the pine trees (*Pinus Khasiana*) and other associated species. They are also fire protected; many animals – leopards, wild cats, civet cats, porcupines, mongoose, foxes, rabbits, hares, and animals of the mole (*Talpidae*) and vole families (*Recefidae*) reside inside them. The jungle fowls, the hill partridges, and the pheasants make these groves their perennial habitat. The two threatened reptiles –-pythons and monitor lizards – also live in these groves.

Unfortunately, however, many tribal traditions and heritage concerning forests and wildlife (benefits from which are now more fully understood through scientific studies) are being given the go-by because of the greed of a few. The small patch of oak-rhododendron – fern forests of the Shillong Peak on very steep slopes represents an unique forest type of the Indian sub-continent akin to the sub-alpine vegetation. The unique vegetation of the Shillong Peak was a sacred grove of the Khasis (Memoirs of Rowntree, last British Conservator of Forests of Assam.) Owing to a unwise greed, the commercial potato cultivators have since the last few years grown potato crops on these undulating steep slopes, almost vertical lines, resulting in the total disappearance of the unique bio-diversity of the Shillong Peak (which used to be a tourist attraction, and a study area for botanists,) but also soil erosion, exposing the parent rocks.

Another example concerning wildlife in Arunachal Pradesh also may be cited here. The musk deer (*Moschuss moschiferus*) is an extremely rare species occurring at very high altitude in Birch forests above the pine zone. They do not live in herds but singly, or in pairs. Only very small numbers are found in Kashmir, Sikkim and at high altitudes in Arunachal Pradesh. Reports are now appearing in newspapers of their being killed in scores by professional poachers, using modern arms – not the traditional bow and arrow – with the assistance of local residents. The musk pods – the source of the highly scented musk – are sent outside India through organized gangs of rustlers. Unless the local population stops aiding and abetting the poachers, the musk deer will soon be extinct.

WILDLIFE IN ASSAM IN MYTHOLOGICAL TIMES

The epic Mahabharata mentions that King Bhagadattwa of Pragjyotishpur sent a large contingent of elephants to help his son-in-law Duryodhan at the Kurukshetra war. The elephants were obviously taken on foot, guided by *mahouts*. From this mention in the Mahabharata, it can be reasonably assumed that even during mythological times, the skills and techniques of catching wild elephants from the forests, and the science and art of training them to obey the commands of the *mahout*, was well developed in ancient Kâmrupa. This heritage concerning taming of elephants continues amongst the Assamese community to this day. Large number of elephant seizers/catchers (*phândis*) and also trained elephants to catch another of their own species is easily available all over Assam. Assam is so well known internationally in having connoisseur in elephant seizing and training maneuver that about two decades ago services of an expert who was a member of legislative assembly, Assam at that time were hired by Government of Malaysia to advice to check elephants' menace in its countryside. The only lady wild-elephant trainer of the world, Ms. Parbati Barua of the Zamindar family of famous Prabhat Narayan Barua and Pramathesh Barua of Gauripur, Assam is a well-known figure in this tricky business of elephant trading. West Bengal Government often utilizes her service to drive back the wild herds of elephants that damage villages and crops in the Bengal–Bihar border, coming from Palamou area. She accomplishes this, not by gunfire and drum beating, but merely cajoles.

Assam has number of Hindu temples, not all of antiquarian origin, but many in ruins. Those, which are in reasonably good condition, show depictions of some animals on the walls and interiors. These animal carvings depict elephants, tigers, bulls and peacocks and thus confirm their existence in this region. Animals similar to lions also appear on the temple walls of Assam, but they are the stylized likenesses only, which corroborates the zoological theory that the climate of Northeast India is too wet for lions to live in.

ACCOUNTS OF EARLY BRITISH EXPLORERS

The British authorities at Calcutta often sent officers to explore the newly annexed land of the Brahmaputra valley in 1826, about which the world knew so little. British army officers conducted the explorations usually singly, taking the help of local people as porters and guides. There is mention of one such exploration conducted by a medical doctor also. The major objectives of these expeditions were to ascertain, whether the Tibetan River Tsangpo discharges into River Irrawady in North Myanmar, or becomes the Brahmaputra; whether the tea plant (*Camellia sinensis*) is found in that part of Indo-China (i.e. extreme northeast India adjoining Burma); how to generally extend the interests of the Europeans by exploitation of the resources of the region? It was confirmed by about 1825, mainly from the report of Lt. Burton that the Tsangpo discharges into the Brahmakund from a perpendicular height of about 'one hundred and fifty feet'. This task was completed in a highly creditable manner in spite of great deal of difficulties, is described by Wilcox (1825) as "with only one surveying compass and unfurnished with instruments for measuring distances and subsequent measurements have detected but little error in the map he made".

Regarding the discovery of the tea plant, following is quoted from the report of Assistant Surgeon, John M. M'Cosh, of Assam Service, dated June 1837.

"Assam with all its wastes and jungles, however much neglected by man has not been altogether forgotten by nature in her distribution of good things of this life. Articles more precious than silver and gold grow wild upon its mountains, uncultivated and till only of late, uncared for. The tea tree, the identical tree of China, grows as favourably upon the mountains possessed by the independent hill tribes, the Kangtis, Singhphos and Muttocks, as in the adjoining provinces of China itself, and it only requires the same attention to be bestowed upon its culture and manufacture to secure the same blessings to our country."

It was also recommended that to achieve this objective, Chinese labour and manufacturers be imported from neighbouring provinces of China. The attempts at importing Chinese labour did not succeed and it is good that labour for the tea-plantations was brought from our own country.

Wild coffee was also reported from several areas in Assam; no large scale plantations were started as plantations of better varieties were started in South India. From about 1960, the Assam Soil Conservation Department has been growing quality coffee by bringing certified seed from the Coffee Board of India.

The early explorers of the 19th Century have not left any detailed account of the forests beyond saying that the flat lands were covered by gigantic reeds (*Ikora, Nal*, wild sugar cane sp., *Khagari* and others) and the hills were covered by forests of deep green leaves, probably *Nahor (Mesua ferra L.), Sia Nahor* (a species of *Family Mesua), Hollong (Dipterocarpus macrocarpus)* and other associate species which occur even now in the regions described. John M'Cosh in his book, *Topography of Assam* (1837) however has included a list of timbers of Assam. The list consists of most of the present-day timber species of Assam (altogether 90 species included). Teak (*Tectona grandis*) obviously did not find a place in the list, as it is an exotic in Assam, introduced in the early part of this century.

The list of wildlife given by M'Cosh is, as expected, far from comprehensive. Some interesting observations however are:

Elephants: plentiful, in great numbers, are caught every season and 700 to 1000 are exported to "other countries " (probably Burma, Thailand and other parts of India).

Rhinoceros: "inhabits the densest parts of the forests". The present management practice of burning the "thatch" and all other vegetation with it every year in March-April in Kaziranga and Manas is contrary to nature and not a scientific practice. In these two parks, rhinos inside woody patches are more healthy, and agile and rarely fall prey to the poachers so easily as in the grassland areas.

Tigers: "numerous but accidents to human life are rare." There used to be Government reward of five rupees for killing a tiger, which the *shikâris* killed by poisoned arrows. The number of tigers killed by *shikaris* was so great that the "amount of reward absorbed a great portion of the revenue."

SHRINKAGE OF FOREST AREAS IN ASSAM

The first major onslaught into Assam forests came during the Second World War, when there appeared food shortages both for the local people and the large number of foreign soldiers stationed in the province to fight the Japanese. Instead of increasing the low yield of the land already under cultivation, the Provincial Government under Sir Saadulla, encouraged immigration from Mymensing and allowed the immigrants to occupy forestland as much as they wished in the name of 'Grow More Food'. Government allowed Lakhs of immigrants to bring large tracts of Unclassed State Forests in the districts of Nagaon, Darrang, Kamrup and Goalpara under the plough cultivation. It is worth mentioning here that frequent floods of the tributaries of the Brahmaputra began to occur since then. Several Forest Reserves were also opened during the fifties ostensibly to rehabilitate flood effected people in North Lakhimpur Districts. The Digboi Forest Reserve was dereserved, ostensibly for the same purpose, but actually many retired officers of the Digboi Refinery were given land for constructing homesteads and farms.

The second major event of forest destruction in Assam was the establishment of a large number of plywood factories in Upper Assam during the fifties. In the first instance itself, 39 factories were established, some of which were the biggest in the country. The owners were all *Rajasthani*s, except two who were from Calcutta. Apparently its objectives were to provide employment to the local youth, and to increase the State's revenue. To obtain more timber for the plywood mills, the existing rules of felling were changed, allowing smaller and younger trees to be cut. The timber was supplied to the mills at subsidized rates, thus incurring a revenue loss for the State. A Government Committee inquiring into the employment aspect reported that the Senior managerial posts in the mills were held by the relatives and friends of the owners, the clerical type of posts were held mostly by Bengalis, and the labour force consisted of mostly Biharis.

WILDLIFE DESTRUCTION

Attitude towards wildlife in Assam prior to 1951 can be judged from the fact that all the sanctuaries were called "Game Sanctuaries" and the animals were collectively called "Game", meaning animals kept for hunting. This writer, in charge of what is now the Manas Tiger Reserve in 1951, suggested to the then Conservator, the late P.D.Stracey that the name "Game Sanctuary" needs to be changed to Wildlife Sanctuary. The suggestion was readily accepted.

The Gazetteer of India of 1965 describes the wildlife situation of the country in the following words:

"Even half a Century ago, it was not unusual to see herds of blackbuck, chital and gazelle as one sped across the countryside in a train. Extension of agriculture to forest lands, excessive hunting, increase of human population and other factors contributed to the decline of wildlife and game. During the two World Wars, game was exploited ruthlessly. Foreign soldiers killed game at will, and completed the process of decline in the abundance of our wildlife".

Though the Assamese people, especially the youth, are now very conscious about protecting wildlife, habitat destruction has become the major threat to wildlife.

PLANTS IN *SATTRAS* AND *NÂMGHAR* PREMISES

The *Neo-Vaishnavite* spiritual leader and social reformer of Assam, Shrimanta Sankardev, established the system of *Nâmghar*s – community prayer halls for religious and social discourses – one in each village, or for a group of hamlets. The *Namghar*s were so constructed as to be able to withstand heavy rainfall and earthquakes – sloping thatch roofs (most now substituted by C.I. sheets as quality thatch is no longer available) resting on timber trusses and rafters. Usually the posts, rather the timber pillars, were of *Nahor* trees (*Mesua ferra*), named Ironwood by the Europeans– huge and majestic, the girth often exceeding three metres or so. This type of construction is now replaced by R.C.C. or brick pillars as trees so huge are no longer available. Efforts should be made to preserve these wood pillars, not necessarily for supporting the roof, but as relics of Assam's forestry heritage. Dilip Medhi informs, "In a few *Nâmghars* at the World's largest fresh water River Island- the Majuli, huge pillars of pine trees are still surviving with a grandiose look. Such types of pillars popularly called the *tulsi khutâ* (pillars of basil plant) are really large enough and are surviving at the *Namghar* of Dakshinpat Sattra. Confusion in identifying the huge columns as *tulsi* ones was based on the pleasant aroma of pinewood. These huge plants were transported from then NEFA, now Arunachal Pradesh" (Personal communication, 2005).

The *Sattras* and *Nâmghars* maintain a serene environment by planting trees which are themselves handsome, and have religious fervour – *Bakul* (*Mimosops elengi*), *Bael* (*Eagle Mermato*), Agaru or *Sâchi* (*Aquilaria agallocha*), *Ashoka* (*Saraca Indica*), *Bot* (*Ficus benghalensis*), *Anhat* (*Ficus religiosa*), *Dimaru* (*Ficus roxburgii*), *Samindh* (*Acasia Siberiana*), *Taruâ Kadam* (*Acasia farneciana*), *Kadam* (*anthocephalus Kadamba*), *Silikhâ* (*Terminalia citrina*), *Âmlokhi* (Emblic; *Phyllanthus emblica*), *Bhomorâ* (*Terminalia belerica*), *Titâsâp* (*Michaelia champaka*) and coconut plant. Assam has a great tradition of making indigenous ink, and papers from the skin of *Sâchi* plant, which entails a grand practice of writing religious scripts including others on the bark of *Sâchi*.   In neighbouring Arunachal Pradesh, religious scripts were written on palm leaf in the Buddhist dominated areas.   These traditions recall an ancient practice of writing scripts in Egypt on *papyrus*, a leaf of some species of *Gramminae* family.   Dilip Medhi who is currently engaged in a research on heritage culture of Northeast India informs this writer, "Thin layers of *Sâchi* plants are first separated and are treated with fresh pulp of turmeric roots and dried later when they become ready for writing inscription.   In ancient Assam, production of scripts on Sâchi bark was an incredible legacy in all the *Sattra*s and *Nâmghar*s, and such scripts are called *sâchi pator puthi*, which are stored in abundance in the *Sattra*s of Majuli.   Upon request, a few elderly devotees at those *Sattra*s can demonstrate the procedure of making a *Sâchi* leaf along writing on it with indigenous ink, which is made with *Silikhâ, Âmlokhi, kechu-rokh* (extracts of earthworm) and *kehrâj or kehrâji (Eclipta alba)*.   We used indigenous inks made with *Silikhâ* boiled in water with charred rice and pieces of iron during our school days at our village Bhawanipur in Kamrup.   Besides *Sâchipat*, *Sattra*s further made *tulâpât* i.e. paper from cotton and also *bhojpatra* from bamboo leaves.   The *Sattra*s in Assam has also a tradition of producing two kinds of heritage dyes- *hengul* and *hytol*; former is a herbal dye whereas *the latter* is made of *lac or shellac crystals* and they were widely used in the illustrations of religious and other scripts, and also in depiction of screens used in heritage one-act play of Saint Shrimanta Sankardeva.   Moreover extracts of earthworm was used in writing secret information on paper by the rulers and others of Assam in the past"(Personal communication, 2005). These institutions and their indigenous knowledge and skills should, therefore continue to play a role in protecting and improving their heritage environment since they enjoy endowments of land from the State and are held in reverence by the people.

THE HERBAL HERITAGE

The Assamese and also the tribal communities of Northeast India or former Assam are great believers in the system of traditional medicine, though the modern medical system is also prevalent. Rural people in many other countries besides India use the traditional medicines. The World Health Organization has recently prepared a manual – "The Use of Traditional Medicines in Primary Health Care" specifically for the villages of the Countries of South East Asia for achieving WHO's resolution to "Provide Health for All" by the year 2000.

Our traditional medicines are mostly derived from different plants and include barks, leaves, fruits and roots of trees, shrubs and herbs. Herbal medicines are reaction-free even after a prolonged use, and usually cure a disease permanently. Some very specific herbal remedies of this region are *Pasotiâ* (*Vitex nigandoo*) against malaria, *Ahui* (*Vitex pedincularis*), the only remedy against *Kala Azar* till Dr Brahmachari released his injection. *Mishimiteeta* (*Coptis teeta*) found in the higher altitudes of Arunachal Pradesh, is highly valued as a "febrifuge", or fever-lowering remedy. Ginseng, the reputed medicine for improving health and vigour are extensively used in China, and now in western countries and has been reported to come from the higher altitudes of Naga Hills.

Moreover there were number of Ayurvedic institutions with *rasalaya*s (medicine factories) in Assam, which were manufacturing a number of quality ayurvedic medicines mostly with varieties of extracts from local plants. These institutions however, could not survive due to a tough competition with the allopathic medicines of today.

CONCLUSION

The tri-junction expanse of India, China and Burma is considered to be one of the world's richest as far as bio-diversity is concerned. Yet it is the least explored. The last botanical explorer who had gone to this isolated tract was Kingdom Ward; he was missing for several days while exploring, because of the dislocation of communications by the great earthquake of 1951. No institution, university or organization is known to have gone on a proper expedition into the region during the last three or five decades, and no important discovery of any flora or fauna has come to light during the period. Mere preservation of bio-diversity for posterity is only one aspect of the subject; investigation and research to obtain chemicals and medicines for the present one or two generations is equally important.

References:

Barbrua, Hiteswar 1997 *Ahom Buranji* (In Assamese). Guwahati: Assam Publication Board.

Gazetteer of India 1965 Government of India.

M'Cosh. J.M. 1837 *Topography of Assam.*

Prater S.H. 1948 *The Book of Indian Animals.* Bombay Natural History Society. Chennai: Oxford University Press.

Unpublished Report, Assam Forest Department.

Waddel, L.A. 1901 The *Tribes of Brahmaputra Valley.*

WHO-SEARO Regional Paper 19. *The Use of Traditional Medicine in Primary Healthcare.*

Wilcox. 1825 *Memoir of Survey of Assam and Neighbouring Countries. 1825. Hill Tracts.*

Mr. Pramod Goswami, a former Indian Forest Service Official was the Former Chief Technical Officer, Food and Agriculture Organization of the United Nations, and, Former Chief Conservator of Forests, Assam

PURÂNAS : THE ASSAMESE TRADITION

Biswanarayan Shastri

Purânas are called the soul of the *Vedas* (*âtma purânam vedanam*). The Indian tradition puts *Purânas* under *dharmasâstra,* which is called *Smriti* in this part of the country - Assam and Bengal. The reason that prompted the law-givers in ancient time is to give *Purânas* unchallenging authority as source of *dharma*, that is after the *Vedas, Smriti* is the means for *dharma*. *Manu*, the ancient law-giver while enumerating the sources of *dharma* puts *Smriti* in the second place.

Vedah Smritih sadacarah svasya ca priyamatmanah/

Etaccaturvidham prahuh saksaddharmasya laksanam//

As Smriti has drawn from the *Purânas* in support of certain views, the *Purânas* may be regarded as a means to *dharma* or source of *dharmasâstra.*

Kumarilâbhatta, the 8th Century commentator on *Sabarabhasya* has dealt with the authority of *Purânas* in his *Tantravarttika* and made an all out efforts to defend certain episodes or instances which go against the socio-religious norms. He defends such instances by providing new explanations or meanings, to them, like Indra's committing adultery with sage Gautama's wife Ahalyâ, Draupadi having five husbands at a time (polyandry), Vasistha's attempt to commit suicide and so on. The attempt to provide new meaning in such episodes is to make them as good conduct or conducts, which is approved by the society.

Historically speaking all the *Purânas* are of later origin, i.e. latter than the *Vedas*. Thus *Purânas* in a wider sense, are elaborate commentaries on the Vedic texts, and it is why *Itihâsa* and *Purâna* are recommended for proper of understanding the meaning and purpose of the *Vedas*. However, there is another view that comes across on the *Purânas* are older than the *Vedas*, and are emanated from the mouth of Brahma.

> *purânam sarvasastrasaram prathamam brahmana smrtam/*
>
> *nityam sabdamayam punyam satakoti-pravistaram /*
>
> *anantaranca vaktrebhyo vedastasya vinirgatah //*
>
> —*Matsya p. 4. 3-4*

Similar views may be traced in the *Vâyu Purâna* (45.20) and the *Brahmânda Purâna* (161.27). Apparently such views go against the tradition that *Purânas and others* have the stories, the germ of which are traceable in the *Vedas*.The utterances may not be accepted in the letters the meaning, which they convey but its significance lies in the spirit of the saying. The meaning of the hidden significance is that *Purâna* tradition is as old, or even older than, the *Vedas*. Though the *Purânas* were compiled in a comparatively later date in historic times, the oral tradition of *Purâna* had been handed down in the society since times immemorial, which with the passage of time had been increasing as and when it was felt necessary. In fact, some of the *Purânas* are seen to contain pre-Vedic tradition and rites.

Again *Purânas* are regarded as the *Vedas* or accepted as the fifth *Veda*.

Itihâsam purânam pancamam vedanam vedah/
- *Chandogyopanisad,*VII.1.2

The *Vishnu Purâna,* the *Vayu Purâna* and *Bramanda Purâna* state almost in the same tune that Vyasa produced the *Purânas (Samhitâs)* out of the materials in the form of *âkhyâna, upakhyâna, gâthâs* and *kalpajoktis* (tradition handed low since long).

Purânas are recognized as a subject of learning in the *Brâhmanas;* the *Satapathabrâhmana* says that on the ninth day in the course of study the *Purâna-veda* is to be taught. The *Gopatha-brâhmana* speaks about *itihâsa-veda* and *Purâna-veda.* The *Purânas* for the ages have been the mines, not only of mythology and cosmic theory of the creation and destruction of the world, but also the fountain head of hopes and aspiration, strength and ideals of the people and the rules for the society.

The *Purânas* are encyclopaedic in contents and exhaustive in treatment of subjects. They are the documents of socio-religious order of the contemporary society, and philosophy of life to be followed by the people of the time and guidelines to the future generation. The *Purânas* used to exercise tremendous influence on Indian minds through the ages all over the country and even abroad. Thus the *Purânas* served as an unifying force. The *Purânas* are always popular with the mass people of this Subcontinent, because they are assessable and intelligible to one and all, because they disseminate knowledge to the people to all start as of the society through popular myths and legends, which directly appeal to the human heart.

This brief preliminary introduction to the *Purânas* is considered necessary to deal with *purâna* tradition in Assam since inception to modern times, because the *Purânas* have been exercising the same influence in the socio-religious structure of Assam as the tradition has been doing in the rest of the country, of course, with local variation.

PURÂNA TRADITION

Similar to parts of the country, Assam built up a strong *Purâna* tradition, and in the process the main stories have been developed with the local tradition and customs. The rivers and hills became holy places of pilgrimage, local heroes and heroines replace the mythical ones, the Cities and Kingdoms have been made clear with the identification of those with that of Assam and ultimately the people become a part of myths. The Assamese society is a mixed one, with Aryan and Austric and Mongolian, and in the *Purâna* myths Aryans and *Kirâtas* and *Mlecchas.* While living with the myths they also contributed certain elements which swell them.

A few mythological events are explained in the following. The 'Naraka myth', the first semi-mythical semi-historical King of Prâgjyotisa (ancient Assam) was born to the mother Earth by Vishnu in His boar incarnation, who made love to her while raising her from the water of deluge; Naraka's defeating the gods, his snatching of the pair of earrings of Aditi, the mother of gods, his collection of sixteen thousand and one hundred damsels of gods, Gandharvas and others; Naraka's killing by Lord Krishna are part of the Naraka myth told in the *Bhâgavata* and the *Vishnupurâna*. These are well known incidents, what is not known is Naraka's birth and his being made the king of Prâgjyotisa. Naraka's birth outside the sacrificial ground of Janaka, that he was brought by the mother Earth disguising her as the nurse Kâtyâyani, that he was brought out of the royal seraglio by Kâtyâyani apprehending divulgence of the secret Vishnu, his putative father, appeared once in the scene and the trio's arrival at Prâgjyotisa journey by river route to Prâgjyotisa, Naraka's fighting and killing, the Kirata King Ghataka, and his appointment as the King of Prâgjyotisa all these events are super imposed and interwoven with the well known Naraka myth in the *Kâlikâ (Upa) Purâna* produced in ancient Assam in 9th Century AD. The instruction given to Naraka by Vishnu along with the description of the land of which Naraka became the King, was noteworthy.

karatoya sada ganga purva bhagavadhisraya!

yavallalitakantasti tavadeva puram tava //

atra devi maghabhaga yoganidra jagatprasuh /

kamakhyarupamasthaya sada tisthati sobhana //

atrasti nadarajp'yam lauhityo brahmanah sutah /

atraiva dasadikpalah sve sve pithe vyavasthitah//

atra svayam mahadeva brahma caham vyavasthitah/

candrah suryasca satatam vasato'tra ca putraka //

sarve kndarthamayata rahasyam desamuttamam /

atra snrvasate bhadra bhogyamatra tatha bahu /

asya madhye sthito brahma prarinaksatram sasarja ha //

tatah pragjyotisakhyeyam puri sakrapunsama /

- K P. 38. 118 -123

This is an instance how a myth of *Satya-Tretâ Yuga* was brought down to *Dvâpara* age and made dear to the people. It is why Naraka is a demon (deity) in the South India and hero with a super human character.

The land grant inscription by Bhâskaravarman (first part of the 7th Century AD) and by the subsequent Kings of ancient Assam begins with a reference to Naraka as the founder of the Bhauma Varman (the son of Bhumi and the Kings were Varman, hence the name) dynasty is ancient Assam. His son Bhagadatta, the friend of Indra (*aham sakha mahendrasya*) who being surrounded by a huge army of Chinese and Kirâtas joined the Kauravas and created havoc. However, he is not described in the *Kâlikâ Purâna*.

Similarly, mythological events and the place where such events had taken place were made to take place in ancient Assam.

MYTHOLOGICAL EVENTS AND PLACES

A few mythological events and places of occurrence have been made near and dear. May be these events had taken place in Assam in the ancient times.

King Bânâsura, the grand son of Prahlâda was the King of Sonitpura. He had a lovely daughter Usâ, who managed to bring Aniruddha, a grandson of Krishna, to Sonitapura through her friend Citralekhâ and kept him confined in her residence as lover.

This place of well known mythology appeals to the people of Assam and indentifies Sonitpur with modern Tezpur in the district of Sonitpur (The Assamese word *tej* means blood so also the Sanskrit word *sonita* means blood, thus Tezpur means Sonitapura).

Rukmini, daughter of King Bhismaka of Vidarbha Nagar eloped with Lord Krishna on the *Svayambara* day. This place of mythology is so dear to the people of Assam that they consider Rukmini their daughter, devoted beloved of Krishna. Here the *bhakti* cult has its influence, a *drama* and a *Kâvya* were composed by Sankaradeva (1449-1568 AD), the Vaishnava preacher of Assam. The legendry belief is that the Kingdom of Vidarbha with its capital city Kundila was in the easternmost part of Assam and they identify a place with a river Kundila in the modern Arunachal Pradesh with Kundila described in the *Harivamsa* and the *Bhâgavata*. The belief is strongly rooted in the mind of the people that no amount of contrary evidences cited against this from the scriptures could effect the belief.

Parasurâma, son of the sage Jâmadagni, visited all the places of pilgrimage after he committed the crime of matricide, to wipe away his sins but failed. The axe remained stuck to his hand, there was no remedy. At last he visited *Brahmakunda*, a holy lake, situated in the east of Assam (now in Arunachal Pradesh) got rid of the sin for committing matricide and the axe having the red coat of blood was also dropped from his hand. The grateful Râma Slashed the bank of the gorge and made its water flow down the valley. The water from Brahmakunda had flown reddish in colour because it became red with the clotted blood of the axe. The river thus emerged through the valley of ancient Assam is called *Lauhitya* (the blood) or Luit. Keeping to the spirit of this mythology every year lots of devotees from different parts of India visit this kunda gorge, popularly called the *Parasurâma Kunda.*

Parasurâma raised a tract of land from the sea, which is called Kerala. He once threw his battle axe to the sea, the land making the limit up to point where it fell in the sea, arose from the water. Thus the country, lying on the north of sea and the south of the Himalayas, from Kerala to Arunachal Pradesh is equally holy to the people who live in this country. This is a *Purânic* way of National integration.

Again the myth of the Brahmaputra, son of Brahma, the mighty river is superimposed on Lauhitya. The story goes on.

Once the royal sage Sântanu, with his wife Amoghâ, had been practicing penance in a hermitage in the Himalayas. One day when Santanu went out leaving his wife alone, there appeared Lord Brahma on his mount swan. He saw Amoghâ young and handsome made a licentious approach to her.

tatrajagama yatrasti amogha santanoh priya /

tam drstva devagarbhayam yuvatimatisundarim /

mohito madanenasu tadabhud dusitendriyah //

udiritendriyo bhutva jighrksustam mahasatim /

- *KP.* 82. 9 -11

Amoghâ could apprehend the intention of Brahma at once, entered into the cottage and shut the door. Brahma was asked to leave the place else he would be cursed. Brahma being thwarted in his evil design discharged his vital fluid on the yard and left the place. Sântanu while returning home found the discharged semen on the ground, understood what had happened. He asked Amoghâ for swallowing the bright fluid, which she refused. At last on the suggestion of Amoghâ, Sântanu himself swallowed it and transmitted the same to Amoghâ who thus conceived. In course of time a mass of water came out from Amoghâ's nostril, and there was a male child within it. He was of red and white complexion, wearing a crown on his head, lotus *vidya* (book) flag and *Sakti* (jevelin) on four hands and was seated on a dolphin.

tanmadhye tanayascapi nilavasah kintadhrk /

ratnamalasamaykto raktagaurasca brahmavat /

caturbhujah padmavidya-dhvaj saktidharastatha //

sisumarasirasthasca tulyakayo jalotkaraih /

- *KP.* 82. 33 -35

Sântanu carried on the mass of water and kept it in a big and deep gorge with four mountains *Kailâsa* on the north, *Gandhamardana* on the south, *Jarudhi* on the west and

Samvartta on the east. After a long time passed Parasurāma visited the lake and had a bath to wipe away his sin of matricide. He cut the bank of the gorge and made River Brahmaputra. Devotee on the 8th day of the bright fortnight of the moon in a waist-deep water of River Brahmaputra recite:

Brahmaputra mahabhaga santanukulanandana /

amoghagarbhasambhuta papam lauhitya me hara //

The story of birth of the Brahmaputra is presented here because it confines to a few *Upa Purânas* while Lauhitya story is an old and popular one. The Brahmaputra myth is superimposed on Lauhitya story to identify the same river by both the names; however the name Brahmaputra is more common and more popular.

Perhaps at an early period the emergence of Lauhitya-Brahmaputra was believed to be from the *Brahmakunda* or *Parasurâmakunda* and later on, the river's emergence was pushed higher to the gorge of the Himalayas and it was linked to the river. The huge volume of water, know as *Lauhitya-Sindhum*, appeared in the imaginative minds of the seers as the son of the creator. What else if it is not directly from the creator.

By referring to myths what want to convey is that the Assamese society had accepted certain myths as told in the *Purânas, Harivamsa* and others, and some of them are found to transform into legends. And the episodes of myths were made part of the early society of Assam, which were much favourite to all and sundry.

This is the early stage of popularity of *Purânas* and their acceptance by the people.

PURÂNAS : LITERARY TRADITION

That myths of the *Purânas* used to exercise influence in the mind of the people, certain events and episodes they have made their own. The mental horizon of the people were fully enveloped by the stories told in the *Purânas*, which are read and explained by a well-versed persons to the common folk. The literature, which is the product of experience and heritage, was reflected in the works.

The earliest documentary evidence could be traced in the land grant inscriptions of the Kings of Prâgjyotisa. The *Dubi* inscription by Bhâskaravarman (598-651AD) draws simile of Balarâma and Acyuta (*Balacyutaviva*); Susthita Varman was born to the queen like Lord Krishna, the destroyer of demons, to Devaki (*krsneneva ca devaki bhâgavata datyanna srimata*). He like Prithu full of all virtues, protected the Prithivi, (*prthyah prthuriva gunah*). His next inscription (Nidhânpur) puts certain similes, which come from the *Purânas*. The King Nârâyana Varman was like Janaka, who acquired the knowledge of *Samkhya* (*janakam ivadhigata samkhyartha*), the King was like *kulacala (kulacalasyeva)*. In the Harjjara Varman's (9th Century AD) land grant inscription are found in very brief allusion to the episode of *Purânas*. "He was put on the throne like Indra by *Marudgana (marudhiriva vasavah)*". Next comes translation and adaptation from the *Purânas*. Factors that promoted translation or the adaptation of *Purânas* may be divided into three categories.

(1)   Need of literature for the mass people or 'pleasure reading' for the people: Though the percentage of educated persons were very limited, the number of intelligible persons was big and they were ever eager to hear stories from epics and *Purânas,* that satisfied their spiritual inquisitiveness.

(2)   Royal patronage to scholars and poets: A few Kings among others, may be cited. Durlabha Nârâyana (13th – 14th Century AD) of Kâmatâpura and his son Indranârâyana; King Mahâmânikya of Varahi kingdom (14th Century AD); King Naranârâyana (16th Century AD) of Koch dynasty of medieval Assam, the Ahom Kings Rudra Simha (17th-18th Century AD) and Siva Simha and Râjesvara Simha (18th AD) are recorded to have patronized learning and scholars. Once the news of patronizing *pandits* by a King was heard, scholars used to block the court of that King. Along with this kind of patronage, the officials and the nobles for dissemination knowledge may be counted.

(3)   The *Vaishnava* monasteries (*Sattra* institutions): *Sattras* are spread over in the Brahmaputra valley, where recitation from scriptures takes place, prompted the scholars to tell the myths in Assamese, the approach of the translator was to remain faithful to the original, and at the same time to avoid theobtruse philosophical discussions, and also to shorten the lengthy description, and to elaborate the ceremonies such as marriage and others, the translators were always aware to know if his Assamese rendering is not difficult to understand by the average listeners. Regarding the use of language they always preferred easily understandable words and expressions, coined from Sanskrit.

One translator says: "The listeners should not denounce me for using words which are difficult to understand, because I use the words to convey the meaning of a passage which deals with profound thought".

pada-artha gambhirata ninda nujuai /
svabhave gahana ito mora dosa nai //

The translator while remaining faithful to the original, substitutes words in lieu of the original by more familiar words, which are associated with the life of the people. For instance, when the cowherd boys tending cows led by Krishna in the summer season were thirsty, *Bhâgavata* says, "One day the cowherd boys of Vrindâbana tending cows felt very thirsty under the Sun of the summer season".

> *atha gavasca gopasca nidaghatapa piditah /*
> *dustam jalam papuh...............................//*

Bhag X. I5.48

Assamese translation reads - *jyestha mâsara raudre pidileka ati /* The word nidagha means summer hot.

Amara says:
nidaghausnopagama usna usnagamas tapah /

Amara, Ist Ka. 18

The Assamese rendering, with a view to make it homely puts *jyaistha mâsa* i.e. the month of *Jeth,* the hot weather in that month has been the daily experience of the people.

In 14th Century AD, we find that certain events and episode from the *Mahâbhârata* were rendered into Assamese. Though the *Mahâbhârata* technically does not come under *Purânas* for all practical purposes this itihâsa has been regarded as the source of *Purânas.*

The scholar-poets who stand out prominently in the early period of Assamese literature are the translators, rather the producer of events, from the epics. Of these early literary figures Hemasarasvati comes first. He was a resident of *Kamagtâmandala,* a Kingdom in the western part of Assam. Hemasarasvati speaks about himself in the colophon of *Prahlâda carita.*

kamata mancala duriabhanara(ya)na nrpavara anupam /

tahana rajyata rudrasarasvati devayani kanya nam //

tahana tanaya hemasarasvati dhruvara anuja bhai /

padabanche teo pracar karila vamana purânacai //

The English rendering of the above quoted passage in "In the Kamatâ *mandala* there reigns the excellent King Durlabhanârayana. In that Kingdom lived Rudrasarasvati with his wife Devayâni, and their son is Hemasarasvati, the younger brother of Dhruva. He publishes this *Prahlâda carita* composed in metrical verses following the *Vamana Purâna*".

Here in this rendering two important issues have come to light, first that the *Purânas* were studied, and stories from the *Purânas* were told by the scholars in the assembly of people, secondly, the selection of *Prahlâda carita* leads to the conclusion that devotion to Vishnu was dominant cult prevailed at that time in the society.

Hiranyakasipu binding no alternative to bring his son Prahlâda to his fold commanded his son, once again to denounce Mâdhava.

hena suni prahlâde sumaranta hari hari /

mâdhavaka mâni gâli pâro kene kari //

mâdhavese pitâ-mâtâ mâdhavese prân /

mâdhavata pare kona bandhu ache ân //

(Prahlâda having heard the command contemplate, Mâdhava is the father, Mâdhava is the mother of all. He is the soul of all who else except Mâdhava is there who is friendly to us).

Hearing this and other arguments by Prahlâda Hiranyakasipu replies. In his reply he hints at the main point.

"Let all live when one (Mâdhava) breathes and let all die when one (Mâdhava) is dead and so forth."

Another poet Harihara Vipra of this period tells the story of *Vabrubâhanara yuddha* and *Lava kusara yuddha* drawn from the *Jaiminiyasvamedha parvan.* That Harihara Vipra has drawn his plot from the *Mahâbhârata (Samhitâ)* by Jaimini proves the currency of Jaimini's work along with the *Mahâbhârata* by Vyasa.

The *Mahâbhârata (Adi. P.)* tells about five disciples of Vyasa, whom he taught the *Mahâbhârata,* and each one of them composed one *Samhitâ* each, the *Samhitâ* by Jaimini is known as *Jaiminiya Mahâbhârata,* though except this *Asvamedha parvan* of Jaimini's *Mahâbhârata samhitâ* is not available. Harihara Vipra has taken the theme of his *Vabruvahanara yuddha* from the chapters 12-14 and 37-40, which is enriched with the side plot of the King Nitadhvaja of Mahismati and his Queen Jvata taken from the same work (Chs. 14-15). Here the fight of Vabruvâhana prince of Manipura, against Arjuna and his army, who followed the horse of *Asvamedha-yajna.* Here the poet follows the original and adds certain descriptions which seem to be needed towards the taste of the local people.

In course of descrption the poet Jaimini states, this fight between Vabruvâhana and Arjuna is similar to that of Kusa and Râma when the horse of the *Asvamedha Yajna* was cought.

Sangramas tatrabhavad-rajan vavruvahana parthayoh /

Yatha kusasya ramasya vajimedhahayedhrte //

In the *Jaiminiyasvamedha parvan* Janamejaya questions in details and to satisfy the questioner, the story of Râma after the death of Râvana is told in brief while the performance of Asvamedhayajna is described elaborately. The description covers from 25th to 36th chapter. These two *Yuddha Kavyas* are from the same work by Jaimini.

In *Lava-Kusara Yuddha Kavya* by Harihara, King Janamejaya suggests even though the two stories are to be heard (in Assamese) please tell *Rama-Katha* first.

Duyo kathâ suniyok mora mana lâge /

Tathapi râma-kathâ kahiyoka âge //

Another poet Rudra Kandali composed a *Khanda Kâvya Satyaki Pravesa,* he has taken the plot from the *Mahâbhârata* (Drona P. 105-107 Chs.) Satyaki, son of Sivi belonging to *Yadu* clan is a great hero and his heroic deeds are described following the text, and the fight between Satyaki and Trigartta, Drona and Dhristadyumna is shortened in the former and lengthened in the latter. The ridiculous sayings by Somakas, Srnjayas and Cedis have been replaced by Assamese abuses.

Another poet Kavi Ratna Sarasvati (not Kaviratna) of this period has composed a *Khanda Kâvya*, namely, *Jayadrathavadha* (assassination of Jayadrath). The plot has been taken from the *Drona Parva* of the *Mahâbhârata*. The poet is faithful in rendering to the original text. Ratna Kandali states that prior to *Jayadrathavadha* he rendered *Adiparva (Mahâbhârata)* into Assamese and composed *Yayâti carita*, where in the episode of Sakuntala occupies a prominent place.

Mâdhava Kandali, who enjoys the reputation of being called Kaviraja Kandali in 14th Century AD rendered Valmiki's *Râmâyana* into Assamese verse. However, *Âdi-Kânda and Uttarâkânda* of this rendering are not available. It is not clear if he rendered only five Kândas only or these two Kândas were lost. It is likely that he rendered only five *kândas* and left out the *Âdi* and *Uttarâ* considering these two *Kândas* are not from the writing implement of Valmiki.

All these scholar-poets of this period, except Mâdhava Kandali, had taken the Mahâbhârata themes and presented them to the Assamese people. Mâdhava Kandali's rendering of the Râmayana into Assamese verses, the earliest in the Northeastern India is remarkable as he faithfully followed the great epic in its original Sanskrit form. There are two more Assamese translations which followed it later.

A landmark in the early medieval literature is the advent of *Neo-Vaisnavism* preached by the great scholar, poet and religious reformer Shri Shri Sankaradeva (1449-1568 AD). Sankaradeva and his followers depended mainly on *Srimadbhâgavata Mahâpurâna* and more particularly on the book and its work. The entire *Srimadbhâgavata* was rendered faithfully into Assamese by Sankaradeva in collaboration with some of his colleagues. The aim and intention of Sankaradeva were completely different from his predecessors. The earlier scholars rendering from Sanskrit epics and new compositions on plots from them were mainly "pleasure reading" and Sankaradeva's and his Vaishnava followers' aim was the "propagation of *Krisnakathâ* and *Krisna (Hari) bhaktî*". Sankaradeva rendered the Bhâgavata into Assamese and adopted many myths in his dramas and treatises separately in independant forms.

(a) *Haricandra upakhyana* – *Mârkandeya Purâna*

(a) *Bhakti-pradipa* (a small *bhakti* treatise) – *Garuda Purâna*

(b) *Uresâ varnana* (description of Orissa) – *Brahma Purâna*

(c) *Rukminiharana Kâvya* (elopment of Rukmini) – *Harivamsa* and *Srimadbhâgavata.*

(d) *Balicalana* (deception of King Bali) – *Srimadbhâgavata* and *Vâmana Purâna.*

(e) *Anâdi patana* (creation of endless world) – *Srimadbhâgavata, Vâmana Purâna.*

(f) *Kirttan-Ghosâ* (poems for recitation by the devotees). Here mainly Krishna's *bâlya lilâ* from the *Srimadbhâgavata,* and His eternal departure to *Vaikuntha* from the *Srimadbhâgavata* and some other *Purânas* are taken.

(g) Of the six *Ankiyâ Nâts* or One Act plays five are with *Krishna Kathâ* - *Râmâyana, Brahmavaivarta Purâna* and *Srimadbhâgvata.*

(h) *(i) Rukminiharana – Srimadbhâgavata, Harivamsa, Vishnu P.*

  (ii) Kâliya damana – Srimadbhâgavata, Harivamsa

  (iii) Râsakrida – Bhâgavata, Vishnu P.

  (iv) Pârijata Harana – Srimadbhâgavata, Vishnu P., Harivamsa

  (v) Râma Vijaya, the Conquest of Rama – *Râmâyana.*

Madhavadeva (1489-1596 AD), the principal disciple of Sankardeva, composed a work, *Namaghosa,* wherein he had rendered about 500 selected verses from the *Srimadbhâgavata* and other *Purânas.* Other post-Sankaradeva writers up to the end of 18th Century followed different *Purânas* for their story or they translated them.

Of the *Purânas* which are frequently referred to or quoted are :

i) *Vishnupurâna,* as shown above is one of the important *Purâna.*

ii) The *Bhâgavata Mahâpurâna,* specially the Xth book of it where the Krishna's myth and His exploits are described.

iii) *Harivamsa* as shown above, Pitâmbara had taken the plot from *Harivamsa* for his *Kâvya Usâparinaya* in pre-Sankara era. Pitâmbara is followed by Gopâla Carana dvija, who composed *pârijataharana Kâvya* on the description of *Harivamsa* supplemented by the Srimadbhâgavata's narration.

iv) *Padma Purâna* is regarded as a sacred *Purâna* by the Vaishnava preachers of Assam, Sankaradeva and his followers had drawn from it.

v) *Brahma Vaivartta Purâna* deals with *Krishna lila* and hence it is accepted as source by the *Vaishnava* saint-poets.

vi) *Vâmana Purâna* was used by Sankaradeva, Pitâmbara and other in their adaptations or creations on the episodes of the *Srimadbhâgavata.*

vii) *Brihannaradiya Purâna* is an *Upa-Purâna,* which was popular with the scholars of Assam . This *Purâna* was rendered into Assamese verse by Bhuvanesvara Misra at the behest of the Kachari queen Candraprabha of Khaspur in modern North Cachar District. A copy of the Assamese manuscript is preserved in the Department of Historical and Antiquarian Studies, Assam, Guwahati (MS.No. 208).

viii) *Kalkipurâna* deals with Vishnu's future incarnation as *Kalki.* This *Purâna* was translated into Assamese verse by Ghanakanta Kharghariya Phukan and a transcript of it is preserved in the library of *Kâmarupa Anusandhana Samiti,* Guwahati.

ix) *Mârkandeya Purâna* is another important *Purâna,* and it contains *Candi,* which deals with the emergence of goddess and killing of *Mahisâsura, Canda-munda* and *Sumbha-Nisumbha*. This *Mârkandeya candi* was translated into Assamese verse by Rucinatha Kandali and two others.

PURÂNAS IN SANSKRIT WORKS

Besides taking episode from the *Purânas'* selected verses relating to devotion of Krishna (Vishnu) are quoted by Sankaradeva, Harideva, and Bhattadeva in their treatises composed in Sanskrit.

Bhakti Ratnâkara, a compilation in Sanskrit on *Haribhakti* by Sankaradeva (1449-1568 AD) contains 39 Chapters. In this work relevant verses from *Srimadbhâgavata, Nrisimha Purâna, Padmapurâna, Brihannaradiya Purâna* and some other *Purânas,* and also other works on *bhakti. Bhakti rasa-tarangini,* a compilations in Sanskrit, on the *bhakti* cult by Harideva (1426-1566 AD) contains 13 *stavakas* (Chapters). In the body of the text the author quotes from the *Srimadbhâgavata, Padmapurâna* and other treatise. *Bhaktiviveka,* a compilation in Sanskrit on *bhakti* by Vaikunthanatha Bhattacaryya who is popularly known as Bhattadeva (1558-1638 AD). The work is divided into 15 Chapters and it draws mainly from the *Srimadbhâgavata* and supporting verses and from 65 works. *Tirthakaumudi* and seventeen other *Kaumudis,* digests on *Smriti* or *Dharmasastra* by Pitambara Siddhantavagisa (16th–17th AD) have drawn profusedly from a number of *Purânas.* This shows the popularity and influence of *Purânas* on the scholars of Assam. For instance, *Tirthakaumudi* (a manual on pilgrimage) draws from the *Padma, Garudâ, Varâha, Linga, Brahma, Kâlikâ, Kurma, Matsya, Brahma-Vaivartta Purânas* and others.

In modern Assamese the *Purâna* tradition can be traced in similes, surprise expression and similar phrases. The few dramas like *Vaidehiviyoga* (separation of Vaidehi), *Nandadulala* (son of Nanda, i.e. Krishna), *Kuruksetra* (the battle of Kuruksetra), *Pârthaparâjaya* (the defeat of Parth i.e. Arjuna), *Bânârâja* (the King Bana), Usa and others are few of many such writings.

Notes & References:

1. *Tantravarttika,* is the commentary on *Sabara bhasya* by Kumarila Bhatta which runs on the second *pada* of the first Chapter, the second and third Chapters of the *Jaiminiya sutra*. The commentary on the first *pada* of the first Chapter on *Sabara bhasya* by Kumarila is called *Sloka varttika* and the commentary on the 4th to 12th Chapters is called *Tuptika*. In *Tantra varttika* (1.3. 1-2) the authority of Smriti on *Dharma* has been established.

2. 1.3.3 *Jaiminiya sutra.*

3. *ibid.*

4. *ibid.*

5. *Satapatha Brahmana,* XIII, 4, 3.13.

6. *Gopagtha Brahmana,* 1.10.

7. *Naraka myth :* Naraka is referred to in the *Ramayana, Kiskindha Kanda, Ch.* 32; *Yuddha Kanda* mentioned in the *Mahabharata Vana Parba,* Chapter 142; *Sabha Parba,* Chapter 38; *Udyoga Parba,* Chapter 48; the story is told in *Vishnu purâna,* Fifth *Amsa,* Chapter 19; *Bhâgavata,* Chapter 29; *Harivamsa; Kâlikâ Purân, a* Chapters 38-41. For details see: Biswanarayan Shastri, Introduction to the *Kâlikâ Purâna, pp.* 154-182; *Naraka Myth,* G.N. Jha Kendriya Sanskrit Vidyapeeth Journal, Allahabad, Vol. XIV, 1993.

8. *Kâlikâ Purâna,* Chapters 383-41.

9. The *Usa-Aniruddha* myth is told in the *Bhâgavata* Chapters X[th]: 62-63, *Harivamsa,* Chapters 117-212.

10. Rukmini's elopment is told among others in - *Bhâgavata,* Chapter Xth: 26; *Mahâbhârata,* Âdi Parba Chapter 67; *Vishnu Purâna, Amsa* 1, Chapter 9.

11. Killing of mother by Parasurâma is a well known myth told in *Brahmânda Purâna,* Chapter 60 and some other *Purânas.*

12. Dubi copper plate Inscription by Bhâskaravarman, 7th Century AD.

Dr. Biswanarayan Shastri, D.Litt., was the formerly Member of Parliament and formerly Vice Chairman, State Planning Board, Assam, Guwahati. Dr. Shastri was an imminent Sanskrit scholar of National and International fame.

DEVADÂSI VILLAGE 'DUBI' IN BAJALI, BARPETA, ASSAM

INTRODUCTION

An effect of religious systems upon the development of a cultural landscape is universally evident. Religious allegiance influences social behaviour because it sets up a particular kind of belief accompanied by a set of norms and regulations. Interaction between people sharing common belief produces distinct spatial pattern that together with their symbolic temple heightens considerable interest in the field of social science researches.

The temple being nucleus of the *devadâsi* village, distance and accessibility from the temple affect the locations of its communities. A close by location helps occupants to nicely tackle socio-religious issues and activities of a temple, and at the same time helps conglomeration of different professional families.

The *devadâsi* tradition attracts attention of mass media, artists and social scientists as well although empirical studies mushrooming up, yet few specialized studies so far been made on the morphology of a *devadâsi* village. Therefore the present effort is likely to go a long way in contributing substantially to the same.

Dubi (26°15'N to 91°5'E) long famed for its *Parihareswar* Shiva temple and its *Devadâsi* institution is spiritually rallying a vast area around the temple. Superbly situated in a stark rural surrounding, Dubi is a couple of Kms. south of Pathsala township and is connected by motorable road. The locality subsided in the 1987 earthquake and therefore the name Dubi- literally meaning 'sink down' was given to it. The temple deity itself lies at a depth of about 3 metres. Dubi-Malipara is the twin villages and according to local legend, the *Parihareswar* Shiva appeared in a mysterious way that resulted in the emergence of these twin villages. In the subsequent time Ahom king Shiva Singha's royal patronage to the presiding deity finally perpetuated the settlement.

Amid a vast majority of *Sudra* population, Dubi remained an island of schedule castes- the *Naths* and *Malis* who appear to be a hybridized form of *Mongoloid* and *Dravidian* populations. These communities came all the way from Dergaon-Negheriting area of Golaghat district at the instance of King Shiva Singha as temple attendants. Physically healthy and attractive as they were, the King made no mistake in finding the beautiful damsel as dancers from amongst them. To perform dance before the presiding deity of the temple was a sacred duty, and which in course of time, created a celebrated *Devadâsi* community in and around the temples' locality. And it is they who brought to the temple a specialized '*Devadâsi* Institution'. This tradition later became the focal point to form a '*Devadâsi* Settlement' in the vicinity of *Parihareswar* Shiva temple.

In 17th Century, during the reign of Ahom King Shiva Singha, various places in Assam namely Hajo, Umânanda, Hatakeswar, Biswanâth, Dergâon-Negheriting witnessed the '*Devadâsi* Institution'. When West Bengal has got its Pather Panchali village; Andhra, its *Kuchipadi* village, why Assam can not be proud of a *Devadâsi* village?

The temple *Parihareswar* is a no work of art, although it was s built on more classic lines. Since the day it was constructed, about four hundred years ago, the temple became the focus of religious life of Assam and the mainland India as well, much particularly with its '*Devadâsi* Culture'. Thoughtful people meet here to invoke its past grandeur, sex-loving men come around to rejoice sex, mothers come for thanks–giving to Lord for having a son. No religious shrine in this part of India seems to have invited such amount of human emotions as that of the Parihareswar temple of Dubi village.

TEMPLE MANAGEMENT AND THE TEMPLE TRIBE

The Dubi village at the periurban location of the Pathsala Township is a temple oriented nuclear settlement. The temple within is more than a home. Its day to day affair is managed by a horde of temple tribe or a management body that comprises– the *Dalai*, the *Pujâri*s, the *Nat*s, the *Mâlâkar*s, the *Âthpariâ*s, the *Bharâli* and the *Mussalman*s. All of them are otherwise known as the Paiks (Temple workers). *Dalai* heads of the temple management. Next come the *Pujâri*s who are the Brahmin worshippers and the Brahmin cooks (*supaker*s). The *Nat*s are of two categories - the female dancers (the *Nati*s) and the musicians (the *Bayan*s). The *Mâlâkar*s, literally means garlands makers, subdivided into four sects - the *Mali*s, locally known as the *Mâliyâ*s, the *Âthpariâ*s (means twenty-four hours duty bound), *Sikdâr Dalai* and the *Thakuria Dalai*. Next comes the *Bharâli*s (Stock keeper) and last comes the Mussalmans or Garia. The Mussalmans are entrusted with the duties of maintenance of the temple drums and also as custodian of the sacrificial animals, especially during festivals. In Upper Assam in *dol*s or temples, a Mussalman family was invariably given a place to stay close to the temple as *Negeriâl* to look after the drums (*Negârâ*) of the temple (Personal Communication through Dilip Medhi with Pradip Chaliha, 2005). Rituals of sacrifice including animal continues till today combinedly offered together to the deities duo- *Pari* (Parvati, the mother goddess) and *Hara* (Shiva or Mahadev) because the latter is considered as the *Ardhanâriswar*. However animal sacrifice (*boli*) is exclusively meant for mother goddess Parvati only.

Temple Tribes And Their Occupations

Serial # Tribes		Sub Tribes	Temple duties
1.	*Dalai*	-	*Head of the Temple Management*
2.	*Pujâri*	(a) Brahmin worshippers (*Pujâri*)	*Worshipping*
		(b) Brahmin Cook (*Supakar*)	*Preparation of temple foods/dishes*
3.	*Nats*	(a) Female dancer (*Natis*)	*Dancing before deity (Twice a day)*
		(b) Male Musicians (*Bayans*)	*To Play Musical Instruments in dance*
4.	*Mâlâkârs*	(a) *Mâli/Mâliyâ*	*To supply flowers to the temple*
		(b) *Âthpariâs* (Temple Manuals)	*Maintenance of sanctity and Cleaning of Temple Premises*
5.	*Bharali*	-	*Store/Stock keeper*
6.	Mussalman/Gariâ	-	*Custodian of temple drums/keeper of sacrificial animals*

Much unlike Hindu villages which are organized on the basis of social class stratification, the *Devadâsi* village was organized on the basis of solemnity of various temple services. People engaged in temple services may be referred to as temple castes. The entire village centres round the temple. All their muscles and mind get oriented in the line of temple customs, its rites and rituals. This has successfully crystallized families into groups, which are hierarchically organized with the *Dalai* at the apex and other *pâiks* including the Mussalmans at the bottom.

SETTLEMENT PLAN

Settlements cluster around the 'Great House' i.e. the temple of *Parihareswar Shiva* takes a compact circular shape. Settlements of each group fairly fall into separate rings. Lanes and sub-lanes between concentric rings of settlement take circular form which together with the cross-roads takes a very well stellar pattern.

The comparative advantages of the settlement areas were assessed and location-strategies were intelligently chosen by the ancient planners and architects. Professionals count low in value move to the distant periphery and that of the high value cling to the focal point i.e. the temple. The temple tribes well justify their indiviidual value, and at the same time, act as the consumers. Agglomeration of temple activities follow a familiar example of clustering for mutual benefits.

The first settlement ring out-side the temple is that of the *Natis* (the temple dancers). In south Indian temples they reside within the temple itself. Since the *Natis* are least movable and as the belief goes they are the choicest people of the Lord and married to him (the Lord or the presiding deity), closely adhere to the temple. They are a specialized group of ladies and become strange beings not allowed to marry any mortal ones since their dedication to the temple is considered them as married to the deity himself. Therefore they are the only female servants who maintain complete *celebacy* among the temple tribes.

The next settlement in the second ring around the temple represents that of the *Bhârâlis* (the stock-keepers) and the *Âthpariâs*. They are entrusted with twenty-four hours' duty. Settlement of the *Mâlis*, is thrown to the periphery since they have the morning duty for a few hours only (collection of flowers from the local gardens including making flower garlands or leis).

The Mussalmans since religiously alien to the Hindus make a separate enclave of their own. Commercial groups of peity traders who sell items of sacrifice to the visiting devotees to the temple are usually excluded, kept in the minimum distance. They are pushed further away from the temple premises because religion is likely to result in material temptation.

Such a cog-web settlement pattern continued with coherence for Centuries together largely because of economic interdependence of temple tribes upon the temple. But with the exit of the *Devadâsi* culture and with the explosive growth of population, the previous settlement pattern disintegrated and lost its previous order. People from the core areas get scattered to the peripheral areas with the passage of time. Although complete ring-forms are not there, a careful observation at the present day villages a few remnants here and there stand to that venerable past.

PLAN OF TEMPLE SERVICES

The temple servants fall into a heterogeneous category, consisting of several occupational groups, wherein each one considers equal to other within the category. Their activities may be categorized to primary, secondary and tertiary. Primary activities are done by the *Mâli*s and the Mussalmans because it is they who produce basic requirements of the temple, e.g., rice, milk, flowers, fruits and vegetables. Secondary activities are done by the *Supekâr*s and *Mâli*s, and, it is they who augment the value of the primary goods as *bhog/prasâd* to be sacrificed to the presiding deity of the temple. Tertiary activities that are connected to the religious fabric of the temple, are performed by the *Dalai* and the *Pujâri*s while the *Nati*s and the *Bâyan*s remain at the top of these kind of services that include management of the temple and the performance of music respectively. Their duties are credited as of highest value that are essential to the system. This also lie, upon bringing in aesthetic behaviours of the temple tribes apart from its command aspect.

CONCLUSION

With the exit of *Devadasi* (which is popularly called *Nati* institution of Assam), the *Parihareswar* temple of Dubi became glamourless and lost all its charisma. The temple tribes have taken to plough cultivation. They are becoming now marginal farmers, landless labour, poor artisans and craftsmen. The whole village, therefore, suffering from a labour surplus and capital scarce economy. There presence of a large size of workforce in agriculture puts an increasing pressure on land. The extent of poverty is much larger than the Lord Parihareswar, to whom the temple community dedicated all their services in the past.

The cultural glamour and opulence of the *Devadâsi* village has, however, gone for ever. Nobody now welcomes the visitors. Its lanes and bylanes, the cottages and bamboo fences, its innocent looking men and women of that glorious past are all quiet. Little more than three decade ago Kausalya, the ultimate member of the *Devadâsi* or *Nati* community was dead. Not a single grieved at her death nor anybody marched to her residence to pay homage to her as the last member of the *Devadâsi* institution at Dubi. Departure of the *Devadâsi* tradition in the Assam Region lost in oblivion due to discontinuation of patronage of this tradition as the Ahom Kings did in the past. The *Devadâsi* in the temples attracted King Shiva Singha to a great deal, who was so much charmed with the beauties of the *Devadâsi* that led him to marry Puleswari, a celebrated *Nati* at the Negheriting Shiva *dol* of Dergâon.

As referred earlier there were many places to have this *Devadâsi* institution and most noteworthy amongst them was that of Hajo. In a conversation with Mr. Pradip Chaliha, a noted dedicated researcher in the field of ancient dance and music of Assam, Dilip Medhi could gather that the form of the music connected to the *Nati Devadâsi* institution could not be properly identified; the *Khemtâ tâl* of the Indian classical music was however confirmed to be associated with this performing dance form. Later during the great *Neo-Vaishnavite* movement in Assam under the leadership of Shrimanta Sankardev, his principal apostle- Shri Shri Madhabdev adopted many of the *Devadâsi* form of music into the fold of their religion and its institution. Another possible reason of departure of this Nati institution was possibly a disparaging status of the *Natis* in the public eye, who with their eloquent beauties remained unmarried in the pretext of they married to the presiding deity of the temple, including their status compared to the prostitutes. Pradip Chaliha observed, this kind of attitude of the modern people of the Indian Subcontinent with a glorious background of past civilization is much unfortunate when great poet Kalidas reported about a form of *Devadâsi* in his classical work- the *Meghadoota* in 4th Century AD and also reference of it existed in 9th Century AD India in Orrissa as *Nashun*, in Southern India as *Dâsi* and *Dolohânganâ* in Benaras (Dilip Medhi: Personal Communication, 2005). More apart, the *Nati* character was also prevalent in parts of Maharasthtra called *Muralis*, *Bâsavis* in Andhra and *Jâgatis* in Karnataka. Finally the *Nati* Institution is a universal phenomenon, which is also reported from the Minerva temple in Greece where beautiful damsel danced before the temple deity.

References:

Chatterjii, S.K. 1970 The Place of Assam in the History and Civilization of India. Guwahati : University of Gauhati.

Fraser, J.G. 1992 *The Golden Bough.* London: MacMillan & Co..

Hunter,W.W. 1886 *Imperial Gazetteers of India.* London: Turbner & Co..

Jena, B.B. 1981 *People Culture and Polity.* New Delhi: Kalyani Publishers.

Sarma, Nabin Chandra. 1997 *Loka Sanskriti* (In Assamese). Guwahati: Chandra Prakash.

Shankar Jogen 1990 *Devadasi Cult : A Sociological Analysis.* New Delhi: Ashish Publishing House.

Weber Max. 1958 *The Religion of India the Sociology of Hinduism & Buddhism.* Glenco: Free Press.

Yinger Nilton. 1963 *Sociology Looks at Religion.* New York: MacMillan.

Mr. Jibal Krishna Patra is a Senior Faculty in the Department of Geography, Bajali College, Barpeta, Assam

INDEX

INDEX

INDEX

INDEX

· INDEX

INDEX

Human Culture, 6
Hymn, 22

I

Ikora, 92
Iliot Smith, 6
In siu, 69
Indo-Aryan, 1, 33
Indological Term, 68
Indo-Mongoloid, 39, 42
Indo-Swiss, 61
Indra, 86, 101, 106
Inorganic, 9
Intangible, 7
Itihasa-Veda, 103
I-tsing, 11

J

Jagadisa Misra, 23
Jagannatha, 23
Jâgati, 71, 83, 128
Jaina Tirthankara
Rvsavanatha, 62
Jainasm, 62
Jainism, 86
Jaintia, 20, 88
Jalpeswar, 40
Jamadagni, 107
Jâmini, 115
Jaminiyasvamedha parvan, 114
Jamuna Barak Valley, 47
Jâpi, 7, 17
Jarudhi, 108
Jayadhwaj Singh, 86
Jayantia, 85
Jethi, 17
Jetuka, 15
Jijiri Kadam, 17

Jogijan, 60
John M'Cosh, 92
Jonebiri, 17
Joymati, 7
Joypiba Lalitaditya, 12
Judhisthira, 87
Juginadi, 70
Juti, 16
Jyaistha Mâsa, 112
Jyoti Prasad Agarwalla, 7
Jyotish, 61

K

K.N. Dixit, 44
Kachari, 88
Kadam, 17, 96
Kardhâni, 17
Kailasa, 108
Kala Azar, 98
Kâlika Purâna, 28, 39, 41, 53, 54, 106, 118
Kâlika, 105, 109
Kâlindi, 23
Kalinga, 59
Kalki, 118
Kâmakshya Temple, 11
Kâmakshya, 10, 37, 39, 41, 42, 53, 56, 65
Kâmarupa, 11, 12, 24, 26, 45, 59, 85, 90
Kâmarupi raja, 11
Kâmarupi, 59, 84
Kamata Mandala, 113
Kanâri Khopâ, 19
Kânbali, 17
Kânda, 116
Kangtis, 92
Kânphool, 17
Karbi Anglong, 43, 57
Karmanâsa, 64

INDEX

INDEX

INDEX

INDEX

INDEX

INDEX

INDEX

INDEX